MW01007045

Working with Culture

How the Job
Gets Done
in Public
Programs

Anne M. Khademian

CQ PRESS

A Division of Congressional Quarterly Inc.
Washington, D.C.

CQ Press
1255 22nd St. N.W., Suite 400
Washington, D.C. 20037

(202) 822-1475; (800) 638-1710

www.cqpress.com

Printed and bound in the United States of America

06 05 04 03 02   5 4 3 2 1

Cover designed by Karen Doody

Library of Congress Cataloging-in-Publication Data

Khademian, Anne M., 1961–
    Working with culture : how the job gets done in public programs / Anne M. Khademian.
        p cm. — (Public affairs and policy administration series)
    Includes bibliographical references and index.
    ISBN 1-56802-687-0 (pbk. : alk. paper)
    1. Public administration. 2. Corporate culture. 3. Performance. I. Title. II. Series.
JF1351 .K487 2002
351—dc21   2002002324

For Gordiya and Yasna
and the memory of their young uncle

Contents

Foreword   vii

Preface   ix

1 Working with Culture   1

   Understanding Culture   3
   Emphasizing Culture in Public Management   5
   The Value of Culture to Public Managers   7
   Going to the Roots of Culture   9
   Culture in Public Programs   10
   Notes   12

2 Culture as a Management Tool: The Debate   15

   The Advocates   17
   The Skeptics   24
   Insights for the Public Manager   33
   Conclusion   35
   Notes   36

3 A Cultural Roots Framework   42

   The Production of Culture   44
   Managing Cultural Roots: Six Strategies for Change   47
   Identifying Commitments   49

Identifying the Connections between the Roots
of Culture and Commitments   53

Determining and Articulating Change   61

Managing Cultural Roots: Inward, Outward,
and Shared Responsibility   65

Being Relentless   75

Capitalizing on and Institutionalizing Change   78

Conclusion   80

Notes   82

4 Extending the Cultural Roots Model   88

Capturing the Essence of Culture   88

The Environment as a Factor: Bank Regulatory
Agencies in the United States   92

Getting at the Roots of Culture: The South African
Police Service   96

Making Changes Stick   101

Conclusion   103

Notes   105

5 Detecting Cultural Commitments: An Exercise   108

Getting a Clear Picture   109

Identifying Commitments   117

Connecting Roots to Commitments   120

Conclusion   121

Notes   122

6 Getting the Job Done with Culture:
Lessons Learned and Questions Unanswered   124

Lessons Learned   124

Unanswered Questions   136

Conclusion   137

Notes   138

Index   141

Foreword

Every new employee starting a new job knows to pay attention to two things: what the boss says and what the office scuttlebutt says about how things really get done. And in every organization there is always a secret lore about who holds the real power, what dress is acceptable, how to win approval of a new idea, and in fact whether new ideas are truly welcomed. This subtle, subterranean sense of how things work is an organization's *culture*. All organizations have a culture. In this important new book, Anne Khademian maps the elements that define the culture of public organizations and considers how this culture shapes public policy. Most important, Khademian asks, can managers use organizational culture as a management tool? Can individual managers reshape culture to transform an organization's results?

Private sector managers have long recognized the importance of an organization's norms and standards in shaping their employees' behavior. Private sector consultants have long developed strategies for helping managers try to shift the culture of their organizations. There has been little work, however, in how these lessons might transfer to the public sector. Indeed, the very question raises the old debate about whether, as former Columbia University political scientist Wallace Sayre quipped, "the public and private sectors are alike in all unimportant respects." In extending the debate to the public sector, what are the broader lessons about organizational behavior—and a leader's role in reshaping an organization—that public managers can use? In this book, Khademian uses evidence drawn from three case studies to argue that skillful public managers can successfully diagnose and transform the cultures of their organizations. She concludes that effective public managers need to acquire and hone these skills.

Working with Culture is an important addition to the CQ Press series in Public Affairs and Policy Administration. In recent years, both the theory and practice of government have come under fierce attack. Reformers point to the need to "reinvent" government and free its managers from dysfunctional processes and structures. Some theorists debate whether the dominant model—hierarchical bureaucracy controlled by authority—still describes how bureaucracies operate. Other theorists seek formal models, driven by game theory, to provide rigor to the discussion. Everyone, inside government and out, worries that government simply does not perform well.

This CQ series aims to produce short, lively, and provocative books that explore the cutting-edge issues in the field. Khademian's book breaks new ground in helping us understand how public organizations really work, what public managers can do to reshape their behavior, and how managers can improve the outcomes of public policy.

Donald F. Kettl
University of Wisconsin–Madison
Series Editor

Preface

The prospect of taking a course on bureaucracy, public administration, or policy implementation seldom engenders enthusiasm among students. A political climate that faults government agencies for red tape and public policy failures can foster skepticism among some students, who question the efficacy of public organizations, and boredom among others, who believe that the real action takes place in the halls of Congress, the West Wing of the White House, and the chambers of the Supreme Court. At the graduate level, students specializing in public policy analysis often view a required course focused on management and organizational concerns as irrelevant to their intellectual development and professional future.

Yet over the years I have found that readings and material from field research, which reveals the inner workings of public agencies, can make these same students both interested in the subject and curious to know more. Beyond the formal mandates, design, and positioning of authority, students are curious about the way the job really gets done. Who are the people working in an agency, and why do they work there? What background and training do they bring to the job, and does their experience matter in what they do? How do line employees relate to top managers? What motivating factors drive the work of employees? How does the agency communicate with the legislature, and what are those communications like? How are directives from the executive or legislative branch received? Are there turf battles, and, if so, who has the upper hand and why? What quirks, oddities, or special features distinguish one agency from another? Efforts to address these questions in the classroom reveal a fascinating political and social world within and between public organizations. More important, students begin to see how organizational factors affect the ways members of the public encounter government and are affected by public policy.

The concept of *culture* captures much of what the students in my courses have found most interesting about the work of public agencies—the informal, the symbolic, the subtle yet nevertheless critical factors that drive the way the job gets done. However, my own efforts to learn more about culture—its influence over organizational behavior and its significance for public policy performance—have been frustrating. Studies range from those that proclaim culture to be a flexible tool that can enhance organizational performance to those that depict culture as a phenomenon so complex and so erratic that students are left scratching their heads and wondering why culture is worth uncovering in the first place. In between is a vast array of analyses that vary not only in their focus and degree of rigor but in the very way culture is portrayed. In short, culture literature is perplexing for the student trying to grasp the concept of culture and its relevance for understanding why government programs don't work better. The literature is also frustrating for the practicing manager looking for a way to improve program performance by changing program culture. This book attempts to address both concerns by building on conclusions drawn from across the breadth of culture literature to explain how cultures form and why they are important and to suggest ways in which public program cultures might be managed. I have tried to capture the complexity, nuances, and intricacies that define culture as a phenomenon, while offering a framework that is both easy to understand and useful for the purpose of understanding and managing public programs.

Although the book draws upon studies of culture in the private sector, its primary focus is the public sector. In writing this book I was particularly concerned with the eagerness of public sector reformers to adopt recommendations for managing culture drawn from the research and experiences of private sector organizations—primarily major corporations. Much of this research is sophisticated in its analysis, and several of these studies stand out for their roles in spearheading a revolution in the study of organizational behavior. But the worlds of a corporate leader and a top public manager are decidedly different. The opportunities, constraints, and expectations that define their respective environments; the source and abundance of their respective resources; and the nature of their respective tasks are fundamentally distinct. Certainly we can learn a great deal from the private sector—and the framework presented in this book allows us to do just that. But in our effort to direct meaningful reform, we cannot ignore the vast research focused on culture in the public sector. Here, scholars are more reticent about the manageability and flexibility of culture as a means to change organizational behavior. We need to understand why this is the case and understand culture in a public context before we can draw upon it as a tool for reforming public management.

The book begins with an overview of the debate between advocates for managing culture and those I refer to as skeptics. I have tried to integrate practitioner-oriented literature with research directed toward academia and to present these diverse approaches in an accessible manner. From this discussion I develop a framework focused on the roots of public program culture and the integration of cultural roots as the key to understanding program commitments—or program culture.

The framework developed here provides students and practitioners alike with the means to develop insights. Students of public administration or public management will find that the concept of culture is intricately connected to program performance and that the tending of culture is an essential responsibility of top managers. Students of policy process will locate public programs in their broader environmental context and connect the roots of program culture to key environmental factors—legislative relations, program clientele, public perceptions of the program, and program legacies. Students of public policy will identify the array of partnerships that work through the connections of culture to implement the details of public programs. Students of organizational theory will note the weighty importance of culture in determining organizational behavior, despite the difficulties of quantifying and measuring its significance. And the practicing public manager will benefit from practical advice about how to detect program commitments and their connections to the roots of culture.

Material to illustrate the framework is diverse. I draw upon a variety of organizations and programs throughout the federal system and across the globe. Three cases, however, are featured prominently: the East St. Louis Action Research Project, the Federal Emergency Management Agency, and the Child Development–Community Policing mental health partnership in New Haven, Connecticut. I chose these cases because they vividly illustrate change in the way work was done under leadership that was sometimes controversial. Whether the changes were perceived as positive or negative, the depth of change in the ways people understood and pursued the work of these programs was dramatic. The cases as they are presented here can do no more than illustrate the potential of the framework as an explanation for culture and as a model for change. But the similar approaches to culture change pursued by the three individual leaders of these three very different programs provide important insights for practitioners set on effecting change and direction for students conducting additional research in public policy.

This book begins with the conviction that culture is a phenomenon worthy of research and of the time and energy public managers devote to its development. The leaders featured here, and the people they worked with, are remarkable for the energy and commitment they displayed to make their programs effective and meaningful in the lives of the people the programs served. Although not everyone will agree that their efforts brought positive change, all readers of this book will be pushed to think in less conventional terms about the factors that drive program implementation and inform public policy performance.

ACKNOWLEDGMENTS

I would like to give special thanks to Don Kettl for his encouragement throughout the writing of this manuscript. His abundant wisdom and perceptive insights provided me with essential guidance and inspiration. My thanks also go to the individuals who offered astute and thoughtful reviews of the manuscript either at the proposal or the full-draft stage: Paul Culhane, Northern Illinois University; Robert Denhardt, Arizona State University; Patricia Freeland, University of Tennessee–Knoxville; Todd R. LaPorte, University of California–Berkeley; Paul Soglin, University of Wisconsin–Madison; Jacqueline Switzer, Northern Arizona University; and Katherine Willoughby, Georgia State University. Martha Feldman's remarkable support and knowledge has helped me to think about some of the concepts in this book through our work as coauthors on several public management papers. The manuscript has benefited from the support of Charisse Kiino, CQ Press acquisitions editor; the superb review and editing of Amy Briggs and Tracy Villano; and the efforts of Sally Ryman, production editor. And my husband, Zarir; our daughters, Yasna and Gordiya; and all the members of my far-reaching family have my eternal thanks for their boundless love and support.

Anne M. Khademian

Chapter

1

Working with Culture

By THE LATE 1980s East St. Louis, Illinois, was by any measure a devastated city. Throughout the 1970s and 1980s businesses and homeowners had moved away, taking with them jobs and the city's tax base. The industrial plants that remained pumped pollutants into the neighborhoods, and industry around the region began to use the city's vacant lots as illegal dumping grounds for heavy metal contaminants. In 1986 the growing financial crisis forced the city to stop collecting garbage. Abandoned lots became garbage dumps. Unemployment neared 25 percent among the 44,000 residents that remained, 98 percent of whom were African American. In some neighborhoods unemployment was nearly 33 percent, and more than two-thirds of the residents lived in poverty. The city owed creditors over $88 million despite severe budget cuts and extreme increases in property taxes.[1] In the midst of trash-filled lots and illegally dumped waste, chemical residue, abandoned homes, drug dealing, and prostitution were "ten thousand desperately poor children living in a dangerous environment, going to shitty schools, told from the day they are born that children of color don't matter."[2]

More than two decades of government programs aimed at stabilizing the economic, social, and environmental status of East St. Louis—from the War on Poverty and Model Cities to the Community Development Block Programs—had failed. In 1987 state representative Wyvetter Younge, chair of the Illinois House of Representatives' Standing Committee on Education Appropriations, took a different approach. When the chancellor of the University of Illinois appeared before her committee for annual appropriations, she requested a demonstration of the university's commitment to urban development for cities like her own, East St. Louis. The university responded with a $100,000 program called the Urban Extension and Minority Access Project (UEMAP). The money supported university faculty and students in the Departments of Architecture, Landscape Architecture, and Urban and Regional Planning to conduct research and design projects aimed at improving conditions in East St. Louis. Three years later more than three dozen projects had been researched and designed, yet only one had been implemented.[3]

1

In 1990 a new assistant professor in Urban and Regional Planning was given responsibility for UEMAP. Professor Kenneth Reardon began by driving three hours to East St. Louis from the University of Illinois Champaign–Urbana campus. He interviewed more than fifty community leaders to find out what they thought of UEMAP. Residents showed little interest in the project. It was just one in a long string of community development efforts that placed power and initiative with policy and research professionals, leaving little to residents eager to organize and participate in the change effort. Instead, residents viewed research professionals as "ambulance chasers" and "carpetbaggers" who used the poverty of the city to secure prestigious grants that brought negligible benefits to the community.[4] In the words of one resident interviewed by Reardon:

> The last damn thing we need is another academic study telling us what any sixth grader in town already knows. Hell, just send us the money and we will take care of our own problems![5]

Professor Reardon found himself at the head of a university–community collaborative effort that wasn't much of a collaboration at all. East St. Louis residents did not participate in the selection or development of UEMAP projects. The emphasis rested firmly on the grand designs developed by university experts but never implemented. In fact, even within the university itself collaboration was not in evidence. The three departments that shared the annual appropriation of $100,000 made no efforts to coordinate spending among themselves.

Professor Reardon set out to transform UEMAP into a vigorous engine for much-needed change. Five years later the renamed East St. Louis Action Research Project (ESLARP) was a thriving, productive partnership between residents, neighborhood organizations, and university students and faculty. With Reardon as lead faculty of the program, residents, faculty, and students worked together to research and develop long-term stabilization plans for neighborhoods throughout the city. They cleared trash-filled lots, rebuilt homes, and designed and built playgrounds. They researched, designed, and built a farmer's market that provided important jobs and fresh produce for residents. They undertook direct and extensive political action to secure parcels of land for community projects. They worked to restart trash collection in the city, and together they documented, photographed, and sampled hundreds of illegal trash-filled lots to begin the massive clean up. Eventually neighborhood organizations newly established as community development corporations were able to secure hundreds of thousands of dollars for additional funding through government and nonprofit sources. A neighborhood college was established to offer any resident of the city two to three courses a semester taught by university faculty on topics ranging from community policing to race relations to economics and municipal government.[6]

What happened in those five years to turn the program into an active partnership of community renewal? The short answer is that Professor Reardon changed the *culture* of ESLARP.

UNDERSTANDING CULTURE

Spend time with people working to implement a public program and a sense of how the job gets done begins to emerge. Participants might hold common understandings of the work they do, why they do it, and how they relate to the clientele they serve. They might refer to and interact with the officials and politicians who oversee the program in distinct ways. They might depict the relationships between people in upper management and those on the line and in the field in particular ways, and hold common perceptions of the ways in which their organization or office engages with other organizations and groups involved in making the public program work. These common understandings could be manifest in a variety of ways, from patterns or styles of communication and language participants use inside and outside of the program to rules of thumb or reference points that guide decision making and help participants to gather, understand, and apply information. They might adopt a common style of dress, share symbols, and organize and decorate working space in particular ways. Stories could be told and retold that help newcomers understand what is important for participants in the program, and why, and help them learn the language, rules of thumb, and understandings of the organization. We can think of common understandings held by people working together in an organization or program as *commitments*. Together, commitments and the numerous ways in which they are manifest form a *culture*.[7]

When people practice or apply the commitments of a culture, they help to define how the job gets done. Consider ESLARP. As we shall see later in this book, participants in the East St. Louis Action Research Project began to share and work with two basic commitments. First, the ESLARP partnership between university faculty and students and the residents of East St. Louis was built upon a commitment to share all responsibility for defining neighborhood problems, setting the agenda, researching problems, and hammering out solutions. Second, ESLARP participants were committed to continuous evaluation or scrutiny of their efforts. Together, these two commitments provided the core of ESLARP's culture under the guidance of Professor Reardon. It was understood that each participant in ESLARP had a responsibility for the research, planning, and execution of projects aimed at improving the quality of life in East St. Louis neighborhoods, and each effort was subject to continuous, intense evaluation to find ways to improve cooperation and program results. These commitments were manifest in a variety of ways. The commitment to shared responsibility was represented in the East St. Louis Neighborhood College, which offered college-level courses to any East St. Louis residents seeking more knowledge or skill in a particular area to improve their capacity to participate. A growing number of computers, technical assistance, and researched databases were made available to residents wanting to contribute to a neighborhood project. And the expectation that faculty members and students would participate in the physical and mental labors of any project reinforced the commitment to shared responsibility. Similarly, the posting of reviews, discussions, and formal evaluations of any ESLARP effort on the ESLARP Web site or in the monthly newsletter represented the commitment to improvement, as did the ritual end-of-the-year meeting focused on critical evaluation of the ESLARP effort on a grand scale. Every dimension of the project could come under scrutiny. These various components and activities of ESLARP highlight the commitments of shared responsibility and continuous evaluation.

In some ways, these two ESLARP commitments provided the essential motivation for participants to tackle difficult problems that had festered for years. The commitments created terms and conditions under which residents could work in an environment of trust with university participants. They allowed participants to remain focused on the day-to-day challenges facing residents, rather than on the eloquence of a report or final research project. And these commitments gave participants a means to persevere in spite of difficulties with the East St. Louis city government and the somewhat tepid support of the university for what was called "participatory research."

Commitments provide a context within which people can interpret and approach their work. Commitments can serve as simple coping mechanisms that aid participants struggling to do difficult tasks with minimal political, financial, and public support. Or they might prompt participants to innovate, collaborate, and improve. Commitments might prove to be functional and facilitate the work of a public program widely recognized for its success in its administration of resources and production of results. Conversely, commitments might prove to be dysfunctional, impeding coordination, limiting innovation, and stalling communication between participants. Commitments might exist in both a coherent package that promotes learning among participants and organizations and in a chaotic package weighted with the residue of past initiatives, longtime efforts to implement complicated laws, and newer initiatives designed to improve service. The commitments of culture can bring odd pieces of an organization or program together and make them gel, or they can clog the works. Yet whether they facilitate or obliterate the work of an organization or program, commitments matter for the quality of what is or is not accomplished. Commitments provide a guide for action and reaction. They are a reference point, sometimes consciously applied, sometimes unconsciously. By their very nature, commitments are deeply imbedded in the work of an office, organization, or several organizations working together.

Yet commitments and the cultures they form can be as elusive as they are important. Commitments won't necessarily be etched in a rulebook or training manual, and not all commitments will be as obvious or as clearly practiced as the commitments of ESLARP. The commitments that drive the work of a public program might not be included in a legislative mandate or even a mission statement. They are, instead, intricately entwined with the day-to-day work of implementing a public program. Commitments arise and take hold because people must find ways to do their job with a given set of resources and skills; coordinate those efforts with other people, offices, and organizations; and do so in a complex environment of conflicting expectations, competing programs, democratic elections, and organizational turf wars. No legislative mandate, no matter how prescient, can clearly specify the way a task should be done under every circumstance, how coordination might best take place, how to navigate political opposition to the program, and how to accomplish it all with limited resources. Instead, people doing the job find ways to get the job done. The commitments that take hold might not be pretty, but they most likely provide confidence and sometimes merely comfort for participants implementing controversial, poorly funded, or politically unpopular programs. Commitments exist because people act upon them and make decisions based upon them. It is through commitments that participants understand what they are doing and why they are doing it.

EMPHASIZING CULTURE
IN PUBLIC MANAGEMENT

Understanding the often elusive cultures of public programs, and why key commitments evolve in any given culture, is an essential ingredient for understanding why government programs perform the way they do. So important an ingredient, in fact, that many recent efforts to reform the way government programs perform focus on culture as a tool that leaders must effectively manage if change efforts are truly to take hold. The reform movements identified as Reinventing Government and Total Quality Management, for example, share a common interest in changing the way resources and power are distributed in organizations and programs. Leaders are advised to create flexible settings where hierarchy and centralized control are replaced by individual initiative, teamwork, continuous efforts toward improvement, competition, and accountability for program results. For many public employees, this formula turns the world upside down. Government employees have often experienced years of going by the book, taking actions only when approved by top management; mistrust engendered by difficult union–management contract negotiations; and a long line of top management initiatives abandoned after just a few months or whenever a new leader arrives. In the case of these recent reform efforts, however, leaders are admonished to rework what are viewed as dysfunctional cultures committed to mistrust, hierarchy, and passing the buck, and to build and manage cultures that facilitate the new distributions of resources and power.

Consider the findings and recommendations of the National Project to Reinvent Government (NPR), a commission established by the White House in 1993 and directed by Vice President Al Gore to facilitate reform of the federal government. Over its eight-year history NPR consistently identified organizational culture as a facilitator of a variety of reforms, from strategic planning to the devolution of authority and the creation of an entrepreneurial spirit in government.[8] In a summary of successful efforts to benchmark, or set performance goals for organizations, the NPR staff reported: "In all cases . . . the culture changed. For effective customer-driven strategic planning organizations, the status quo is simply not an alternative."[9] The transformation of public organizations from stagnant, top-heavy bureaucracies to flexible, flatter organizations that respond to "customers" or clients, in other words, requires managers to create a supportive culture.[10] Managers able to build a supportive culture—in this case, a culture built upon commitments to teamwork, innovation, customer service, and the importance of results—are able to offer employees an alternative way to think about, approach, and conduct the work of government.

This interest in culture as a management tool is not unique to public management. In the past decade or two, culture has become a focus for business leaders. For more than a century reformers and political leaders have looked to the world of business to inform public sector improvements, admiring the efficiency of business organizations and the abilities of business leaders. In the early 1900s Progressive reformers were heavily influenced by Frederick Taylor's model of "scientific management" as a means to improve government efficiency and to ensure neutrality in government administration.[11] Reformers have long assumed that business organizations under contract with the government can produce government goods and services more efficiently than the government itself.[12] And the current reform language of strategic planning, customer service, bottom lines (that is, performance), and continuous improvement has its roots in the private sector.

The emphasis on culture as a management tool is no different. Efforts to analyze and harness the cultures of organizations highlight the importance of culture to performance.[13] The business world has embraced culture as the key to promoting excellence in organizations spread across the globe, struggling in competitive and volatile markets, and defined by decentralization and teamwork.[14] When the work of a business is fraught with uncertainty and complexity, it is culture that provides employees with a " 'thick' and shared social knowledge" that helps them to understand the organization's objectives, methods, and values.[15]

It is precisely the uncertainty and complexity of work in many public programs that makes managing culture an attractive possibility for improving government performance. If business leaders are able to manage culture toward more productive ends, why not leaders in the public sector as well? But the interest in culture as a public management tool is more than an imitation of business. It also reflects frustration with past reform efforts, a frustration shared by organizational scholars and public managers alike.[16] In the past thirty years public managers have participated in many reform efforts, including management by objectives, performance program budgeting, zero-based budgeting, and decision making based upon cost–benefit analysis. The primary objective of these reforms was to rationalize the management of public programs by requiring agencies to be clear about their objectives, precise about their financial needs given these objectives, and more exacting in their decision making. While some of these reform efforts linger in the work of public organizations, most have gone by the wayside.[17] However, today reformers argue that the key to reform is a change in culture— the less tangible and less formal dimension of an organization that can support or sabotage change.

Finally, the "right" culture is considered an important ingredient not only in facilitating reform efforts but in providing managers a source of control and accountability in more decentralized organizations. An organization built upon a strict hierarchy concentrates control with leaders and top managers. Decisions are made at headquarters rather than in the field or on the line. But an organization flattened by reforms, with decision-making power spread to individuals and teams throughout the organization, will require different systems of control. An organizational culture that communicates clearly to members how things are done and how they ought to be done could go a long way in guiding the work of an organization without tight central controls.[18] A culture in which members accept and exercise decision-making authority at all levels of the organization will communicate a commitment to individual responsibility for decisions and the outcomes of those decisions. The same culture might also promote open communication throughout the organization to facilitate oversight by top managers, as well as promote innovation and improvement.

THE VALUE OF CULTURE TO PUBLIC MANAGERS

For all of the fanfare and optimism, very little is known about how public managers might actually use culture as a tool to improve government performance. A real change in culture might be obvious, but knowing how to bring about change in the first place is not always clear. Replacing old commitments with new commitments intended to motivate and guide members to do the work differently is surely a complicated task. Can something so abstract and elusive be managed in a public organization or program, and, if so, does it really matter for performance? If public managers look to the business world for answers to these questions, they will receive an enthusiastic "yes" to both. As discussed above, a growing number of business scholars and practitioners argue that building and maintaining an effective culture should be the number one priority of a top manager or leader.[19] Managing a culture is not only possible, it is essential. Books focused on culture as the key to achieving high performance in organizations identify the ideal culture as one that integrates work throughout an organization, making a seamless connection between different divisions and regions, and even creating a cohesive bridge between possible subcultures throughout an organization.

At the same time, however, organizational theorists and political scientists are emphatic in stating that managers *cannot* change the culture of public organizations. Organizational cultures are recognized as very real and very important for the way organizations do their work. But any effort to change or manage culture in a public organization will most likely fail. The dominant determinants of a culture, such as the political and historical context, the professional training and orientation of employees, the task at hand, and the fiscal and political resources available, will usually overshadow any manager's efforts to bring about change. Hence, cultures in public organizations will grow like vines around a tree, tight and tangled, their primary goal one of reaching the sun, one of survival. While they may be quirky and dysfunctional, they will nevertheless help the members of the organization navigate the context in which they must conduct their work. Top managers must simply learn to live and work within the cultures they inherit.

In Chapter 2 we will see that, although the proponents of both sides of this debate recognize the critical role culture plays in organizational performance and the difficulty any top manager faces in trying to transform a culture, they reach different conclusions about the capacity of a leader to actually build or change a culture. The problem is, the two sides arrive at their respective conclusions by looking at two distinct worlds, with differing evidence from each. Much of the enthusiasm for managing culture comes from the world of business, while the more sanguine assessments are often based on work in public programs. And those who view culture as manageable focus on the actions of top business leaders, while those who view culture as more permanent and unbending focus on the structural and environmental features of public organizations. To this point, reformers have borrowed heavily from the world of business to make the case for managing culture. And why not? Advocates for managing culture in the public sector argue that what works for business should work for the public sector, because differences between the two worlds are increasingly less significant. Both public and private organizations operate in complex environments with fluid goals. Both must meet or deal with the expectations of numerous stakeholders in their daily efforts.[20] But significant differences remain. Public managers work within systems over which they have little control. Rules for hiring, firing, and promoting employees; rules for contracting; and rules for budgeting and spending money are all specified by law. Even the tools managers use and the way the tools can be employed, from strategic planning to goal setting and benchmarking, are often mandated.[21] And increasingly public managers must partner with a variety of public, private, and nonprofit organizations to bring public programs to fruition. The constraints faced by a public manager in tackling something as complex and intrinsic as culture are significant when the tools and systems of management can create obstacles rather than offer flexibility.

GOING TO THE ROOTS OF CULTURE

In Chapter 3 we will examine a framework for understanding and managing the roots of culture in public programs. The framework builds on two premises. First, the commitments that form a culture result from the collective efforts to conduct a particular public program or task using a specific set of resources and skills, and to do so in complex political, historical, and economic environments. The environment of every public program is a unique combination of political oversight, competing and overlapping programs and jurisdictions, public perceptions and understandings of the program, economic conditions, and historic precedent. These factors will present obstacles and opportunities for the conduct of a public task, as will the skill set and resource base available to a program. Employees trained as lawyers will approach any given task differently than employees trained as economists or engineers. Unionized employees will have different incentives and concerns than nonunionized employees. The differences are not trivial. Employees bring to a public task not only skills and knowledge but also a specific worldview or paradigm, applying particular thought patterns and questions to the focus and interpretation of program responsibilities and the day-to-day conduct of the task. And the task or tasks of any given program can vary in important ways.[22] Some tasks are straightforward, with a clear set of guidelines for determining whether or not the task is being done well and clear observable indicators of how well individual employees are performing. Other tasks are difficult to define, dependent upon expertise to administer, and hence very difficult to assess. As in the case of resources and the environment, these differences are not trivial. The ways in which employees pursue any given task, with particular resources and skills, and do so in the context of changing political, social, and economic environments, will form the basis or the roots for program commitments.

The second premise of the model presented in Chapter 3 is that public managers as leaders don't manage culture per se. Rather, they can influence and help shape commitments by managing the process of integration or the way the roots of culture weave together. In order to change a culture, a leader must work with the roots of culture and try to influence the ways in which the roots connect and don't connect to organizational commitments. This means working on how the tasks of the public program are understood within the program and how program resources and personnel are applied to the task, as well as focusing on key elements of the environment that impact the evolution of program commitments. Leaders then must focus management efforts on both the inward elements of a program and on the outward dimensions of a program such as relationships with political overseers, public understanding and perceptions of the program, and relations with other organizations or programs. As we will see throughout the book, the effort to manage the integration of cultural roots must be relentless. A leader must practice the changes they would like to bring about and continuously work outwardly and inwardly to maintain those changes.

Professor Reardon led a remarkable culture change in ESLARP by going to the roots of the UEMAP culture. He confronted and challenged the professional approach of faculty participating in the UEMAP program. He and his ESLARP associates fostered efforts to challenge the city government of East St. Louis rather than remain "above" political engagement. They resisted the pull and influence of other university programs. Reardon changed the rules of engagement with residents and the process of identifying problems, developing and implementing stabilization plans, and evaluating success. And his persistent presence in the city, and that of his colleagues and students, built trust and demonstrated commitment to the project, which in turn encouraged greater participation.

Throughout this book programs as diverse as ESLARP and the Police–Mental Health Partnership in New Haven, Connecticut, and organizations as disparate as the Federal Deposit Insurance Corporation and the Federal Emergency Management Agency will serve as models through which to illustrate the framework. The examples offer readers a means to think about the roots of culture in a variety of public programs, and the role of public managers in managing the integration of those roots.

CULTURE IN PUBLIC PROGRAMS

In some respects, the success of ESLARP might seem an odd example with which to introduce a book on culture in public programs. The program is based in a university campus. It is focused exclusively on the challenges facing neighborhoods in a single city and is implemented as a partnership with residents of that city. And the program is not contained in a single organization, but rather is spread among an amalgam of neighborhood organizations, churches, on-site offices, classrooms, city and state government programs, and units of government. But these characteristics of ESLARP represent a trend in public policy toward local solutions, broad participation, and public and private sector partnerships.[23] The dimensions of the ESLARP program can help guide us in understanding the culture of public programs and the role public managers as leaders can play in producing positive results.

The potential leaders of culture change in the public sector are a diverse lot. When we think "public manager," we typically envision the head of an organization or division within an organization, educated in public affairs from budgeting to policy analysis, and detached from politics in his or her management efforts. In the case of ESLARP, Kenneth Reardon was an unlikely public manager: a university professor, responsible for a program combining public university resources and numerous neighborhood and nonprofit organizations. Reardon's efforts involved mobilizing and organizing partners, and in some instances taking direct political action to bring about policy change. His willingness to work outside the traditional boundaries of a university–community partnership—building partnerships and challenging political leaders and institutions inside and outside of the university setting—was key to the change of culture in ESLARP.

Public managers today are likely to be partners in a leadership effort, such as culture change. Reardon was a leadership partner in ESLARP. At the heart of the UEMAP culture was a hierarchy of expertise: university faculty members were perceived to have it and residents in a distressed inner city not to have it. At the heart of the ESLARP culture was a commitment to broad-based participation and shared expertise: everyone participates, everyone has something to contribute, and everyone can learn something from someone else. In this spirit, Reardon partnered with other faculty, community leaders, students, residents, and anyone else committed to the ESLARP effort. Rarely did Reardon use the word "I" in describing his work with ESLARP. In fact, he might have objected to a portrayal of his efforts as a "leader." Instead, the term "we" was used with great deference to the residents and other participants. In a world of increased collaboration across organizations, governments, and sectors, public managers today must find ways to work with other leaders in a variety of settings.[24] The culture of these efforts, we will see, is a critical dimension for public policy performance, and the ESLARP example sets a precedent for how a culture of shared responsibility might evolve.

Rather than focus exclusively on the cultures of single organizations, in this book we will refer to the cultures of public programs. In some instances the culture we examine will be that of a single organization. In other instances the culture will be that of a program that crosses and links a variety of organizations. The framework presented in this book can be applied to either setting. The broader, more collaborative world of public policy requires an equally broad, more collaborative understanding of the culture that evolves to fill in the cracks within an organization, settles amidst the legalese in a contractual arrangement between organizations, and roots within memorandums of understanding and handshake agreements between partners in public policy.

ESLARP's culture was distinct. It oriented new faculty, students, and residents participating in the project. It guided the steady stream of careful evaluation cast upon every project and plan by participants. And it sustained an atmosphere of hope in the midst of despair. Within the culture of ESLARP, residents, faculty, and students hammered, painted, dug, scraped, photographed, documented, analyzed, collected, planned, evaluated, marched, testified, learned, and learned more side by side. The culture was the consequence of a professor's initial vision, and that of several East St. Louis residents, of what collaboration could be, mixed with the skills and experiences of all participants, the political and historical contexts swirling around the program, and the daunting task before them.

Like ESLARP, every culture is unique, sometimes odd or quirky. Yet more than just a quirk or curiosity, culture is a vital component of the way public programs perform. Indeed, one cannot read a book, article, or government publication focused on reforming government without finding "culture" cited as the key to effective reform.[25] And in those same publications top managers or leaders of the public effort are invariably charged with changing that culture. We will see, however, that such approaches to culture and culture change in the public sector are somewhat shallow and underdeveloped. Rather than borrow *carte blanche* from the world of business, reformers must adopt a new framework within which to understand and manage the culture of public organizations and programs. The framework presented in Chapter 3 is an attempt to consolidate what we already know about managing culture and build on it to help us better understand and manage culture in the public sector. The approach treats the concept of culture as commitments that guide the way work is done. In so doing this book will no doubt offend and possibly outrage many that view culture as unmanageable and infinitely complex. Culture is complex, absolutely. And there is much about culture that is slighted or ignored in this book. But the essence of what is manageable about culture is well represented by the concept of commitments. Further, if culture is to be manageable, a shorthand is needed, albeit one with deep roots, for busy managers responsible for complex and vast programs in the public sector.

Chapter 4 offers a defense and an extension of the framework presented in Chapter 3. Chapter 5 walks the reader through an exercise in identifying cultural roots and commitments in a public program, and Chapter 6 identifies the basic lessons we can draw from the model and the examples, and the questions that still need to be addressed.

The mission of this book is to examine what we know, what we can learn, and what we still need to know about efforts to manage the culture of public programs. The suggestions offered here, based as they are on the real-life experiences of today's public managers, should go a long way in achieving more effective management of culture in tomorrow's public programs.

Notes

1. See Kenneth Reardon, "Back from the Brink: The East St. Louis Story," *Gateway Heritage* (winter 1997–1998): 5–14; and Reardon, "Enhancing the Capacity of Community-Based Organizations in East St. Louis," *Journal of Planning Education and Research* 17 (1998): 323–333.

2. Kenneth Reardon, telephone interview with author, November 3, 2000.

3. Rep. Wyvetter Younge secured $900,000 from the state's Build Illinois Program to build a manufactured housing factory. Reported in Reardon, "Enhancing the Capacity of Community-Based Organizations," 325.

4. Kenneth Reardon, "Participatory Action Research and Real Community-Based Planning in East St. Louis, Illinois," in *Building Community: Social Science in Action,* ed. P. Nyden, A. Figert, M. Shibley, and D. Burrows (Thousand Oaks, Calif.: Pine Forge Press, 1997).

5. Quoted in Kenneth Reardon, "Creating a Community/University Partnership That Works: The Case of the East St. Louis Action Research Project," *Metropolitan Universities* (spring 1995): 47–59.

6. Ibid.

7. The term *commitment* is Philip Selznick's. See Selznick, *Leadership and Administration: A Sociological Perspective* (New York: Harper and Row, 1957), 38–56. Selznick argues that a "character" or culture evolves that is manifest through "the elaboration of commitments—ways of acting and responding that can be changed, if at all, only at the risk of severe internal crisis" (p. 40).

8. Al Gore, "The New Job of the Federal Executive," *Public Administration Review* 54 (1994): 317–321.

9. National Performance Review, *Federal Consortium Benchmark Study* (Washington, D.C.: Government Printing Office, 1997), 3.

10. Michael Barzelay and Babak Armajani, *Breaking Through Bureaucracy: A New Vision for Managing in Government* (Berkeley: University of California Press, 1992), esp. 132.

11. Frederick Taylor, *The Principles of Scientific Management* (New York: W. W. Norton, 1911). For a discussion of Frederick Taylor's influence upon Progressive reformers, see Jack Knott and Gary Miller, *Reforming Bureaucracy: The Politics of Institutional Choice* (Englewood Cliffs, N.J.: Prentice-Hall, 1987), 55–76.

12. See, for example, President's Private Sector Survey on Cost Control (Grace Commission), *Report on Privatization* (Washington, D.C.: Government Printing Office, 1983).

13. Edgar Schein, in *Organizational Culture and Leadership* (San Francisco: Jossey-Bass, 1985), offers one of the most rigorous efforts to research culture and apply the analysis to the management of culture.

14. Terrence Deal and Allan A. Kennedy, *The New Corporate Cultures* (Reading, Mass.: Perseus Books, 1999); and Thomas Peters and Robert Waterman Jr., *In Search of Excellence* (New York: Harper and Row, 1982).

15. Alan Wilkins and William G. Ouchi, "Efficient Cultures: Exploring the Relationship Between Culture and Organizational Performance," *Administrative Science Quarterly* 28 (1983): 468–481.

16. Organizational scholars, too, have come to focus on the culture of organizations as an essential ingredient in understanding why organizations behave the way they do. Like government reformers, these scholars have grown frustrated with predominant theories of organization to explain, predict, or diagnose organizational actions. In his study, *The Organizational Culture Perspective* (Chicago: Dorsey Press, 1989), J. Steven Ott argues that some scholars reject the emphasis on organizational structures and systems as the key to understanding organizations because "such methods have produced very little useful knowledge about organizations over the last

twenty years" (p. 3). The study of organizational culture brings with it a primarily qualitative methodology for examining and explaining the behavior of organizations, rather than quantitative methods.

17. See, for example, James Fesler and Donald Kettl, *The Politics of the Administrative Process*, 2d ed. (Chatham, N.J.: Chatham House, 1996), 261–262.

18. William Ouchi, *Theory Z: How American Business Can Meet the Japanese Challenge* (Reading, Mass.: Addison-Wesley, 1981).

19. Schein, *Organizational Culture and Leadership*.

20. Mark Moore, *Creating Public Value: Strategic Management in Government* (Cambridge: Harvard University Press, 1995), 68–69.

21. For example, the Government Performance and Results Act of 1993 mandates government agencies to set goals for performance of federal programs, to measure the performance of those programs, and use performance information to improve results. As described by the General Accounting Office (GAO), agencies are required to submit strategic plans that include "mission statements, general goals and objectives, strategies for achieving goals, key external factors, and a description of the actual use and planned use of program." General Accounting Office, *Managing for Results: Building on Agencies' Strategic Plans to Improve Federal Management*, Testimony before the Committee on Government Reform and Oversight, House of Representatives, Statement for the Record by James F. Hinchman, GAO/T-GGD/AIMD-98-29, September 16, 1997, 3.

22. See James Q. Wilson's discussion of production, procedural, craft, and coping organizations that vary in regard to whether the people conducting the activities can be monitored or observed, and whether the results can be clearly observed, in *Bureaucracy: What Government Agencies Do and Why They Do It* (New York: Basic Books, 1989), 158–171.

23. Edward Weber, *Pluralism by the Rules: Conflict and Cooperation in Environmental Regulation* (Washington, D.C.: Georgetown University Press, 1998); Barry Rabe, *Beyond NIMBY: Hazardous Waste Siting in Canada and the U.S.* (Washington, D.C.: Brookings, 1994); and Steven Rathgeb Smith and Michael Lipsky, *Nonprofits for Hire: The Welfare State in the Age of Contracting* (Cambridge: Harvard University Press, 1993).

24. John Bryson and Barbara Crosby, *Leadership for the Common Good: Tackling Public Problems in a Shared Power World* (San Francisco: Jossey-Bass, 1992).

25. See, for example, David Osborne and Ted Gaebler, *Reinventing Government: How the Entrepreneurial Spirit is Transforming the Public Sector* (Reading, Mass.: Addison-Wesley, 1992); Al Gore, *From Red Tape to Results: Creating a Government that Works Better and Costs Less,* Report of the National Performance Review (Washington, D.C.: Government Printing Office, 1993).

2

Culture as a Management Tool
The Debate

FOR MUCH OF THE TWENTIETH CENTURY the challenges of managing public programs were met with structural, technical, and rational solutions. In the early 1900s Progressive reformers advocated new, "scientific" personnel systems that utilized standardized testing and evaluation for hiring new employees and evaluating existing employees. "Each job," one historian wrote, "could be scientifically analyzed to show its 'functions' and 'responsibilities.' Each function and responsibility could be given a precise mathematical weight corresponding to its importance in the overall job. And the success of the employee in each function and responsibility could be given a precise mathematical grade."[1]

In the 1930s Luther Gulick wrote what would become the definitive statement of structure as the key to efficient and effective government performance.[2] Writing for the Brownlow committee[3]—established to advise and support President Franklin Roosevelt's efforts to reorganize the executive branch—Gulick argued that organizations should be built around a specialized task and further subdivided into specialized units with work performed by specialized employees. These specialized organizations, he stated, should be tightly constructed as hierarchies with authority concentrated in the hands of individual administrators. And administrators at each level of the organization should have narrow spans of control to facilitate control over subordinates. The resulting structures, he argued, would be neutral in their function, making the work of government efficient and effective.

Yet, as the endless efforts to restructure government and individual programs suggest, attention to structure and process alone might not be sufficient to enhance the quality and effectiveness of public programs.[4] Like an orchestra performing a symphony, implementation of a government program has an internal rhythm, pulse, or tempo. A conductor focused only on the composition of the musical score, the placement of instrument sections, and the seating of musicians based upon their individual skills would not likely produce the passionate performances of the world's best orchestras. Between the musical score, placement of instruments, and musicians are gaps that must be filled with understandings and communication between the musicians and the conductor. How to read a piece of music, how to interpret a passage or string of notes, and when to look to the conductor for guidance, to the first chair of an instrument section, or to proceed on one's own all facilitate the production of a musical performance.

Implementing policy in the public sector is no different. Between the formal structure, the definition of process, the allocation of authority, and the location of employees are gaps that gradually fill with culture—understandings of, or commitments to, how the work is done. Even the most sophisticated, reengineered systems require a bit of oil between the gears to help participants proceed in a climate of uncertainty. Mayors, governors, and presidents begin each term with an agenda for change. Populations transform. Budgets grow and shrink. Interest groups support and oppose. Legislatures and city councils create new mandates. Partnerships are made and broken. Top managers come and go. But members of the public must receive veterans' benefits, garbage must be collected, airplanes must travel safely, borders patrolled, library books loaned, and parks maintained. Participants in these efforts learn lessons to cope with uncertainty, and those lessons can become commitments, which in turn are essential to how the job gets done and hence very resistant to change.

Scholars and practitioners in the public and private sectors have long recognized culture and its importance for organizational performance.[5] There is disagreement, however, as to whether culture can be *managed* to facilitate performance precisely because of its stamina and durability. Indeed, the beauty of focusing on structure and process as primary management tools is that they are concrete. Regardless of culture's importance, if it can't be changed or managed, why bother? In fact, why not eradicate old cultures with new structures? But culture can be sticky and spread from one system to the next if the task, participants, and environment remain the same.

In this chapter we will examine the debate over managing culture. Advocates for managing culture make their arguments from a private sector perspective, focusing primarily on the efforts of a single leader. What happens within organizational boundaries is their area of interest. The environment as a root of culture is overlooked. Government reformers have borrowed liberally from this literature. In contrast, skeptics of the private sector approach focus on factors other than leadership to determine the roots of culture and consequences for behavior. Their areas of interest encompass both the public and private sectors, paying careful attention to the environment of an organization. Government reformers have largely ignored this literature. Both sides offer valuable insights that will aid in developing an alternative framework for thinking about and approaching culture management in the public sector.

THE ADVOCATES

A vast and disparate literature focused on organizational culture teems with disagreements over what a culture is, how to identify culture, how it influences organizational behavior, and how to examine culture to better understand it.[6] A relatively small but critical portion of this literature is focused specifically on culture as a management tool. Yet even within this portion of the literature differences abound. Some studies begin with hypotheses about connections between culture and performance and end by presenting methods with which to find answers.[7] Others draw upon case material and the researchers' own experiences to cull lessons for managing culture.[8] Some aim to understand and develop theory about organizational culture, its evolution, and significance,[9] while others seek to offer leaders and other top executives simple guides for getting a handle on organizational culture.[10] Regardless of the approach, many of the advocates are consultants, assisting small and large companies alike to understand and manage culture. And virtually all the advocates can trace their intellectual roots to the work of Chester Barnard, the president of New Jersey Bell in 1938.[11]

At the heart of Chester Barnard's book, *The Functions of the Executive,* is a simple but compelling insight. Barnard argued that executives trying to organize people for a common goal must overcome one basic obstacle: self-interest. Executives must find a way to match individual interests with the interests of the organization, or motivate people to put the interests of the organization over their own.

The primary tool for this task, Barnard argued, is the personality of an organization, or the "points of view, fundamental attitudes, [and] loyalties" of members.[12] A strong personality (or culture) can motivate members of an organization to put the good of the organization above individual self-interest. Organizational personality can, in other words, harmonize and integrate work, and it is the "distinguishing mark of executive responsibility" to build and maintain a personality that supports the work of the organization.[13] When reform efforts in business and government were focused on the rationalization of structure, technical solutions, specialization, span of control, and process, Barnard was focused on culture as key to performance and as a tool of motivation and control in the hands of a leader. If understood and used effectively, he argued, organizational personality could be more effective than the exercise of sanctions, the implementation of structured processes, or the use of material rewards.

Today's culture advocates argue that attention to organizational personality or culture is not only more effective than sanctions, structure, or material rewards, it is essential for making organizations competitive in the global market and harmonious in the face of lightning-fast change in the workplace and economy. The first wave of culture advocacy followed several years of economic decline, oil price increases, and significant competition from Japan in the late 1970s and early 1980s.[14] The competitive advantage, it was argued, required attention to the cultures of U.S. companies to create more flexible and innovative work environments. Today the primary concerns are mergers and acquisitions, corporate downsizing and outsourcing, and the spread of technologically connected employees across the country and globe—all factors that tug and tear at a coherent corporate identity.[15] Some business leaders view culture as a way to control this changing workforce and organizational sprawl. Others are seeking in culture a way to enrich the human experience of working for a particular company. Whatever the motivation, today's business environment has propelled the concern with culture to the stature proposed by Chester Barnard. Two fundamental arguments embedded in today's advocate literature are directly connected to Barnard. First, a unifying culture can be used to weave together the work of an organization and enhance performance and, second, the top priority of a leader is to mold and maintain a unifying culture.

An Integrating Force

Because it integrates the work of an organization, culture, advocates argue, matters—and matters a lot—for performance.[16] Scholars have noted, "A company can design a great product, build it flawlessly, market it inventively, and deliver it to market quickly. But to do that year after year is a function of culture—the organization's underlying social architecture."[17] The right "social architecture" or culture is believed to provide a means of managerial control, as well as employee identification, loyalty, motivation, and coordination.[18] A strong, integrated culture is essential for the physical and mental well-being of employees.[19] Advocates argue that a culture can give strength and, when necessary, flexibility to organizational procedures. A culture internalized by members of an organization can guide action in the face of unforeseen circumstances in a manner consistent with a mission.

Culture is manifest in a variety of ways. Many advocates focus on some combination of "values," "beliefs," and "basic assumptions" that serve as the "bedrock" of an organizational culture.[20] Massachusetts Institute of Technology professor Edgar Schein is the dean of this language. He established a theoretical framework for understanding organizational culture as three layers of organizational interaction (see Figure 2.1). The deepest level of culture consists of basic assumptions that capture fundamental notions of how the organization and its members relate to the environment, time, space, reality, and each other. Basic assumptions are taken for granted and below the level of consciousness for most members of an organization. This is the heart of culture and motivates behavior.

Figure 2.1 Schein's Three Levels of Culture

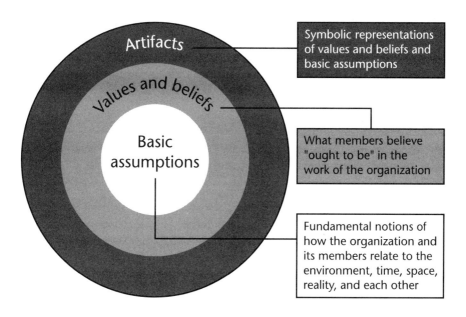

To arrive at this deep root of culture one must traverse two additional layers that are more visible in their manifestations and extensions of the basic assumptions. The middle layer consists of values and beliefs, or what members believe "ought to be" in the work of the organization. Ideologies, attitudes, and philosophies are found within this layer and are more readily examined and scrutinized than basic assumptions. A culture might promote the belief that all employees should have the opportunity for continuing education and training, or the attitude that the customer is always right. Others might embrace the idea that all members of the organization ought to be treated like family.

Finally, at the most visible level are cultural artifacts—the language used, stories told, ceremonies performed, rewards given, symbols displayed, heroes remembered, and history recalled. An organization that believes work should be accomplished through broad and diverse participation might organize the workspace to facilitate open communication, to remove signs of hierarchy between employees, and encourage a dress code that promotes equality among participants.

Any effort to manage culture must first comprehend these three layers and their relationships to each other. Ultimately, leaders must not approach culture as a superficial phenomenon. Before culture can be changed, deeply held, basic assumptions must first be changed.

Many advocates are less formal in their description and identification of culture. What are labeled cultural artifacts by Schein are identified by others as the basic elements of culture—symbols, stories, heroes, special language, rituals, and ceremonies.[21] Still others look for patterns that emerge in organizational design, communication, perceptions of time, and organizational identity.[22] Whether theoretically robust or casually descriptive, however, advocates imbue these various dimensions of culture with the potential to integrate work within a corporation. For advocates, culture is akin to commonly held focal points that not only facilitate internal cooperation, but contribute to an overall reputation that other organizations, shareholders, or customers can use to assess the organization as a potential partner, agent, or producer.[23]

Advocates for managing culture disagree, however, on the specific characteristics of culture that bring about integration and benefit an organization (see Table 2.1). While some argue that there are specific common characteristics of a culture that promote excellence or competitiveness, others argue that it is simply a matter of robustness (that is, the depth and duration of a culture). Still others view a capacity to adapt and learn as the essential integrative feature of a culture.

Contrasts between the cultures of American and Japanese companies in the 1980s pointed to a particular formula or set of cultural characteristics that would integrate work. A 1981 study argued that American organizational culture embraced hierarchy, individual specialization, responsibility, and decision making (Theory A). Coupled with an emphasis on short-term employment, American cultures promoted distrust and conflict between management and employees and inhibited innovation and change. Japanese firms, on the other hand, utilized clan control, or control based upon a social understanding of the organization's objectives, methods, and values, rather than hierarchy (Theory J). Specialization was low, employment considered lifelong, and responsibility for outcomes and decision making shared among all organizational members. Taking the best of both worlds, Theory Z proposed a corporate culture built upon clan control, long-term employment, limited specialization, individual responsibility, and consensus-based decision making. This combination of cultural characteristics fostered teamwork and innovation to facilitate change and success in a more competitive global market.[24]

Narrowing the focus to "America's best run companies," others identified what they understood to be the key dimensions of successful cultures.[25] Specifically, cultures promoting excellence in performance fostered simple, lean organizational structures that allowed closeness to customers and placed value on autonomy and initiative among individual workers. These companies had a "bias for action," practiced "hands-on management," and could "stick to the knitting," or the primary purpose of the organization. Most critically, cultures in these companies were tightly held, allowing the company itself to be loosely and flexibly organized. The culture integrated or tied the pieces together.

Table 2.1 What Makes Culture an Integrative Force?

Integrative Attribute	Characteristics of the Culture
Promotion of excellence	A culture that promotes excellence values individual initiative and responsibility, as well as groups or team decision making; also features simplicity, or limited specialization.
Robustness	It is not necessarily the particular features of a culture, but the depth with which members of an organization hold dimensions of a culture. A robust culture has a long history, maintained by members of the organization through the roles they play, stories they tell, language they use.
Capacity to adapt and learn	A culture promoting a concern for all stakeholders; a belief that change is possible; a commitment to trying new things, learning, and trying again; and a commitment to teamwork, diversity, and systemic thinking.

This last dimension, the strength of a culture, is the focus of other advocates. Successful companies don't necessarily possess the same type of cultural characteristics. Rather, successful companies have strong, or robust, cultures. "A robust culture is committed to a deep and abiding shared purpose."[26] It is a tapestry of corporate history, values and beliefs, rituals and stories held together and strengthened by members of the culture who play distinct roles in maintaining cultural robustness. It is, in other words, well integrated. Changes in the business landscape make such tightly held, exclusive cultures all the more important for top performance and innovation.[27]

Robustness, too, has been challenged as a prime feature of successful cultures. In its place an adaptive culture, or one that promotes learning, has been offered as most likely to facilitate a company's long-term performance in a competitive global economy.[28] Adaptive or learning cultures help companies anticipate and adjust to changes in the environment by simultaneously paying attention to the demands and concerns of customers, shareholders, employees, and members of the community. These cultures send the message that the environment of an organization can be changed, and members of the organization control the destiny of the organization. Learning as an organizational activity is valued by the culture, and the culture supports the opportunity for employees to learn, make mistakes, and learn some more. Finally, learning cultures are thought to embrace open communication, diversity, teamwork, and systemic (or nonlinear) thinking.[29] Robust cultures, however, can inhibit change that is necessary in today's global and rapidly changing economy. While a strong culture might provide employees with vision and motivation, and perhaps the solution to recent or future short-term success, it might also make a company inward-looking, arrogant, and even bureaucratic in its focus, inhibiting the capacity to change in the long run.

Whether cultures are strong or weak, adaptive or bureaucratic, or representative of numerous other typologies, the search for the forces that can integrate the work of an organization goes on.[30] An integrative culture can pull together disparate offices, locations, specialties, and employees to focus on the task at hand and to meet new challenges in a global economy.

The Importance of Leadership

The second basic argument advocates draw from Chester Barnard is that a corporate culture can be managed, and responsibility for managing culture rests with the top executive. "Successful reorientations" of corporate cultures are attributed to "active, dynamic, and visible leadership" that can "capture and mobilize the hearts and minds of the people in the organization."[31] Some argue managing culture is the single most important responsibility of a top executive.[32] Accountability for culture rests with the most senior leader because she or he is the primary contact with the organizational environment and representative of the organization.[33] While none would argue that managing culture is an easy task, advocates definitely view it as a possible task for leaders with great commitment.

An organization's original leader, particularly a charismatic leader, is recognized as having significant influence on a culture.[34] In addition, the leader of an organization still in its formative years—someone seeking to hone and implement the mission and identify goals and constituencies—or a leader during a time of crisis could also significantly influence an organizational culture.[35] For example, in 1935 James Landis was named chairman of the Securities and Exchange Commission (SEC), the New Deal agency created to regulate the buying and selling of stock (securities) in public markets. Landis, an attorney and author of the SEC legislation, believed regulation of stock exchanges and other security markets was best achieved through full disclosure of information about publicly traded companies and tough enforcement of the securities laws. His insistence upon rigorous statutory interpretation established standards of legal expertise few government agencies could match and facilitated successful court actions when the agency sought to enforce securities laws. At the same time, Landis was reluctant to develop rules to regulate the securities industry and have the rulemaking authority of the agency challenged in court. This commitment to legal remedies and legal excellence, as well as guarded use of rulemaking authority, remains today a strong feature of the SEC culture.[36]

Few leaders have the opportunity, however, to begin building cultures from scratch. Instead, most begin with established cultures that they can try to change, maintain, or strengthen.[37] Advocates offer leaders a range of recommendations for assessing the culture of an organization to determine what the culture is, and how changes in the culture could facilitate work in the organization. Leaders might begin by stepping back, or marginalizing themselves from the daily routines of a company to see a clear picture of the culture and their role in it, as well as to assess the environment of the organization and potential barriers to any culture change.[38] In their assessment efforts, leaders should focus on the ways in which the current culture is communicated through the use of symbolic behavior, language, the stories told and how they are told, and the role of routines and special events.[39]

The SEC provides a great example of symbolic behavior. For years the five commissioners of the SEC, including the chairman, rode in an old station wagon when getting around town or traveling to Capitol Hill for hearings or discussions with members of Congress. The action was symbolic, communicating a message of thrift, seriousness, and civic duty to employees of the commission as well as to Congress and the industry it regulated. The securities industry, or any other source of political influence, would not sway the regulatory decisions of the SEC. In later years, the story of the station wagon was told to communicate the same message about the agency and its legacy. In this serious, civic-minded environment, the commission letterhead once read, "Good People, Important Problems and Workable Laws." For the leader of the SEC, the symbolism embedded in the station wagon story and the language of the letterhead serve to communicate the culture of the SEC.

In their writing and consulting efforts, advocates offer a variety of specific tools intended to identify and assess a culture. These range from questionnaire surveys and interviews administered in an organization to exercises aimed at diagnosing organizational responses to surprises and critical incidents or to hypothetical situations.[40] Some simplify the world of possible cultures into four types, offering leaders models for thinking about the ways in which their organizations are similar to or distinct from a given type.[41]

Once the appropriate cultural form is identified and an assessment is made, advocates propose ways in which leaders might change the culture. Some concede that the task of culture change is considerable, requiring the "words and deeds" of leaders, including "redesigns or reconfigurations of the organization's processes, structures, and resource allocations"[42] The package of words and deeds recommended by the advocates is extensive. Others suggest that leaders "discover and articulate distinctive ideologies" and "recruit like-minded people." As chairman of the SEC in 1981, John Shad put both levers to work to try to change the long-standing culture and ultimately the regulatory focus of the agency once influenced by James Landis. He consistently articulated a vision of less regulation over the securities markets to enhance competitive forces and capital formation. The approach cut directly against the disclosure and enforcement ideology that guided the agency for more than forty years. Shad also aggressively recruited like-minded people. Rather than draw upon legal expertise, he created the Office of the Chief Economist and hired economists whose work emphasized free market competition. Economists began participating in the decision-making process, offering advice and discussion points at commission meetings. The actual office of the Office of the Chief Economist was located near the chairman's office on the top floor of the SEC building.[43] John Shad's physical placement of the Office of the Chief Economist and his invitation to advise and confer with commissioners was a direct effort to manage cultural forms, or symbolic structures. Advocates also urge leaders to be clear about what is important in the new culture and what is not, what will be monitored and controlled, and what will be rewarded and punished.[44] The formal structure of an organization that establishes divisions, job descriptions, pay, and promotion can be managed to break up the social dimensions and work habits of the old culture and facilitate new working arrangements. Leaders can redefine short- and long-term goals and choose to give priority to one or the other.[45] Leaders define culture by what they "pay attention to, measure and control" and how they handle crises, allocate rewards and sanctions, recruit, promote, and deal with retirement and even excommunication.[46]

But ultimately the longevity of a change effort rests with the persistence of a leader to use these various levers until changes take hold. Implementation, say the advocates, is everything.[47] John Shad was persistent in his six-year tenure with the SEC. Shad could not change established job descriptions, organizational divisions, pay and promotion throughout the agency. Civil service, statutory guidelines, and members of Congress stood in the way. He could, however, pay attention to the analyses and recommendations of the economists rather than the attorneys, and he could elevate the stature of the economists by placing their office close to his own and inviting them to participate in commission decision making. While the clout of the economists and the free market emphasis of the agency waned after Shad's departure, his tenacious focus on implementation left an indelible mark on commission culture in the form of a solid seat for economic theory in commission decision making.[48]

THE SKEPTICS

Are leadership efforts the primary influence over the culture of the SEC, or for that matter of any private or public organization? The advocates' arguments discussed above form a mere slice of the rich and vast organizational culture literature. Many who have studied the subject have reached different conclusions as to what a culture is and how it influences performance. In fact, most students of culture would conclude that the culture of an organization is *not* manageable. Political scientists, sociologists, and anthropologists alike acknowledge the power of culture in determining organizational behavior but believe that culture is highly resistant to the change efforts of leaders. It is not that skeptics view leadership as having no influence at all. On the contrary—like the advocates, skeptics believe that leadership in the formative years of an organization exerts a great deal of influence on culture.[49] But other cultural determinants are deemed weightier. In his analysis of six government bureau chiefs, Herbert Kaufman writes of the frustration leaders face in trying to bring about change:

> Each new leader after the first one enters an organization with a history of managed learning permeating its personnel. To be sure, the methods by which past learning was instilled in the work force may be used to introduce new patterns of behavior also. But it takes time and resources to effect such changes. . . . A new chief is therefore likely to feel sharply constrained by what was deliberately infused into his work force by his organization before his accession to office.[50]

As the quote from Kaufman indicates, skeptics believe that the accumulated efforts to perform the task of an organization—with particular resources and particular employees—are crucial in determining how work is done. The nature of the task and its interpretation and pursuit by organizational employees weighs heavily in explanations of culture and its inflexibility.[51] But perhaps most critical to arguments of the skeptics is the connection between the environment of an organization and its culture. Numerous factors outside of an organization or program can influence the way the job gets done. For a public organization or program, politics and political institutions are paramount. The conduct of oversight by the legislature, relationships with the executive branch, organized groups with an interest in the policy area, and the power and voice of the clientele served by the program all impact the way in which a program is implemented.

Just as important, but more difficult to characterize and study, are the perceptions, understandings, and systems of meaning held by members of a community or society that guide the interpretation of what a public program is supposed to accomplish, and why. Perhaps the complexity of what constitutes an environment limits interest in it among advocates as a variable of central concern to an organizational leader. The environment is instead viewed as something to be monitored and, if necessary, adjustments in the culture can be made to fit it.[52] Among skeptics, however, a vast number of factors in the environment directly influence culture, and changes in the environment can be reflected in the culture. It is this overwhelming environmental influence that prompts skepticism about the manageability of culture. Referring to research that identifies the environment as key to the formation of culture, one scholar writes, "The implication, of course, is that *we cannot understand what goes on inside an organizational culture without understanding what exists outside the boundary.*"[53]

The Importance of Environment

Skeptics differ in the ways they interpret the connections between environment and culture. One prominent interpretation describes culture, in part, as a reaction to the environment. In some cases culture emerges as a means to navigate complex and uncertain environments.[54] In others, the culture is no more a vehicle for safe environmental passage than a leaky boat in rough seas. In either case, the culture is buffeted and dented by changes in the environment.[55]

A Navigation Tool. The sociologist Philip Selznick argues that organizational cultures (or "characters") evolve in response to the uniqueness of the organizational task, the clarity of organizational goals, and the availability of standardized information to conduct the work of the organization. Some organizations can be maintained as machine-like tools "[w]hen the goals of the organization are clear-cut, and when most choices can be made on the basis of known and objective technical criteria." Organizations that have no competitors in their environment, however, whose goals are not clear, and whose work depends heavily upon subjective criteria develop organizational "commitments—ways of acting that can be changed, if at all, only at the risk of severe internal crisis."[56] Commitments, the term adopted here from Selznick's work, become the means by which organizations navigate uncertain environments.

Like the advocates, Selznick views these commitments as a source of "social integration [for the organization] that goes well beyond formal co-ordination and command."[57] But it is precisely because culture evolves to deal with environmental uncertainty and complexity that it is very difficult to manage, or even budge. "[A] wise management will readily limit its own freedom, accepting irreversible commitments, when the basic values of the organization and its direction are at stake. The acceptance of irreversible commitments is the process by which the character of an organization is set."[58]

For many scholars of the public sector, the political environment is the primary influence upon an organization's "irreversible commitments." Public agencies in the United States operate amid the uncertainty and complexity of a federal political system, competing branches of government, strong and active interest groups, changing public and private partnerships, and continuous changes in leadership. Organizations must find a way to navigate this environment. The evolution of organizational commitments could reflect these navigation efforts. So powerful can the environmental demands, constraints, and uncertainty be that the commitments evolved to navigate the environment become granitelike.

One study of the State Department captures the dominance of environment over organizational culture and the difficulties faced by leaders trying to "unfreeze" organizational commitments.[59] The study examines the efforts of one leader to eliminate a highly bureaucratic structure and culture in the 1960s by decentralizing operations in portions of the State Department. Referring to members of Congress with "de facto ownership" of various operations in the State Department, the study found that "a major barrier to unfreezing, and a crucial prop for existing structures, is the perception that a change effort will be thwarted by mortgage holders in the agency's power setting."[60] Here, merely the *perception* that change would be thwarted was a powerful organizational commitment that inhibited real change and maintained the power of politicians in the political environment over the daily operations of the State Department.

Some skeptics argue that organizational commitments not only appear "irreversible" to public managers, but can also act upon and influence the way managers manage.[61] In complete contrast to the advocates, these authors see organizational commitments defining what is possible for public managers rather than the other way around. This conclusion is reinforced by a five-case study of federal managers where both line and staff managers were guided in their efforts to negotiate the budget and civil service systems by the norms and incentives of their agencies.[62]

Fragmented Culture and Environments. Not all skeptics view culture as a means by which to navigate complex environments. Some authors view culture as the manifestation of multiple and fragmented meanings that change constantly and create ambiguity for organizational members.[63] Changes in the environment can bring about changes in the culture that simply contribute to the ever fluctuating, ever fragmenting nature of culture. Advocates view organizational symbols, ideology, and organizational actions as promoting harmony or integration. Those who see culture as fragmented and ambiguous, on the other hand, believe that consensus over how work is done, even at lower levels of the organization, can change at any time, creating new understandings or simply ambiguity.[64]

Among these authors, changes in the environment are understood to be a common source of change in culture. In the public sector presidents and governors are elected, undertake new initiatives, and make sweeping changes in bureaucratic leadership; new mandates are handed down from legislatures; courts overturn the policy status quo; and natural and man-made disasters strike and strain organizational processes. In an analysis of studies that view culture as fragmented, one scholar writes, "These studies . . . do not assume that people can control, or even influence what happens." [65] Organizational cultures respond with changes in organizational symbols, ideology, and action. But the changes are not systematic, focused, or rational. They are mixed, chaotic, and difficult to decipher. Members of the organization then experience inconsistencies between the symbols, ideology, and actions.[66] An organization that emphasizes equality in its ideology, for example, might nevertheless allocate office space on the basis of title or salary; or an organization whose leader emphasizes interpersonal communication to facilitate cooperation might nevertheless communicate strictly by memorandums that pass through the hierarchy. Such ambiguities reflect the constant interaction between the environment, the organization, and members throughout the organization.

Symbols and Systems of Meaning as Environment

The environment is often thought of in physical or concrete terms. A political environment, for example, consists of formal structures such as a legislature focused on holding an organization accountable and promoting responsiveness to the public interest. Public programs operate in the environment of mandates, rules, and regulations; formal institutional arrangements between an organization and the legislative, executive, and judicial branches of a government; organized groups that participate in the activities of an organization; and other organizations participating in the implementation of a program.

The relevant environment for an organization can be viewed in terms of the symbols or systems of meaning that shape and influence the way the job gets done within the organization.[67] Symbols—a flag, a song, a style of architecture, a cross, or a statue—convey meaning to members of a society, be it a small town, a region, or the country as a whole. Systems of meaning also provide context and meaning to societies. The terms *efficiency, gross domestic product,* and *free trade* and the words *liberty, freedom,* and *rights* convey a set of ideas to observers or listeners. A system of meaning is a construction of ideas that forms an understanding of a specific phenomenon and serves as a guide and system of motivation for behavior. Liberal or conservative political theory, free-market economics, our definitions of "public problems" and our explanations for why the problems exist—each is a system of meaning within which individuals interpret the world.

Symbols and systems of meaning are critical components of an organizational environment, exerting a great deal of influence on how the work of an organization is done. This influence might be unconscious, seeping into or saturating the organization and dominating the way the organization is managed and pursues its task, or conscious. Organizations might adopt a symbol or way of thinking about a particular policy as a means of gaining legitimacy or prestige in its immediate environment. Finally, systems of meaning can influence culture when they accompany professionals closely identified with the work of an organization. By default, design, or transplant, systems of meaning are important components of the organizational environment (see Table 2.2).

Influence by Default. Some skeptics argue that dominant systems of meaning or ideas from outside an organization permeate efforts to manage or establish a unique culture within an organization. An example of this sort of influence is the effort to build "quality" cultures within organizations as part of the total quality management (TQM) reform effort. Like the advocates, TQM reformers view culture as an integrative force, manifested as strong commitments to "quality" principles championed by organizational leaders and adopted by organizational members. TQM's central premise is that it is the quality of a service or product that is of paramount importance.[68] Empowered employees who focus

Table 2.2 How Systems of Meaning in the Environment Can Influence Culture

	How It Works	Examples
Default	A dominant system of meaning outside an organization penetrates the way work is organized and the way members understand and pursue their work	The system of meaning emphasizing quantity rather than quality The system of meaning surrounding drunk driving
Design	An organization adopts a system of meaning or adopts symbols of the system of meaning to confer legitimacy upon the work of the organization or to be in sync with the adopted system	The establishment of consumer protection regulations in banking The creation of policy analytic offices in government agencies
Transplant	Systems of meaning become part of a culture when the professionals or members of a particular industry or group bring a set of ideas and concepts to bear on the work they do. The system of meaning is particularly influential when expertise is exercised with a high degree of autonomy	The influence of economic and banking expertise as systems of meaning within the Federal Reserve Board

on continuous improvements in results (services or products) produce quality for their customers. Empowerment includes the freedom to innovate and license to occasionally fail in good faith efforts to achieve quality. The work is incremental and from the bottom up, focused on the details of executing each and every job (and each component of every job) as the means to achieve superior quality and, ultimately, organizational success (profitability).

This quality organizational ideal is held out as a replacement for the "quantitative" organization that seeks a hedge against insecurity by emphasizing growth for economies of scale. In the quantitative organization, rationalization and specialization of tasks are thought to enhance hierarchical control over people and processes and, above all, efficiency (rather than quality).[69] Critics, however, argue that the quantitative system of meaning, focused on growth and the bottom line, can never really be replaced. As a dominant environmental force, it simply absorbs and modifies the effort to impose a culture of quality.[70] In their study of a public ferry organization, Virginia Hill Ingersoll and Guy Adams argue that the culture of quantity continues to linger in organizations bent on quality reform. Eventually the emphasis upon the rationalization of work, the means rather than the ends, hierarchical control, and the importance of efficiency above all else will suppress the empowered employee and the organizational commitments to quality.[71]

Systems of meaning in the environment influence the way work is approached and conducted in other compelling ways. For example, changing attitudes towards drunk driving have affected the work of police departments and other public organizations responsible for enforcing safe driving laws. Over the past thirty years the public meaning of drunk driving has changed from a ticketed offense to a deviant, morally delinquent act considered more criminal than speeding or reckless driving. Accident statistics, analyses connecting high blood-alcohol levels with accidents, and a well-organized political campaign to both preempt drunk driving and increase the penalties for drunk driving have worked to alter public perceptions of the offense.[72] This system of meaning is now part of the environment for police departments charged with enforcing traffic violations as well as for other public organizations charged with enforcing safe driving laws, and its influence upon these organizations is twofold.

First, the system of meaning attached to drunk driving provides motivation and guidance to the work of police officers, judges, probation staff, and employees of state departments of motor vehicles and secretary of state offices charged with licensing drivers and registering cars. The way these agencies interact with individual offenders, the guidelines they follow (both formal and informal) for punishing the offense, and the educational approach they might take to prevent drunk driving will all be influenced by the evolved system of meaning defining and judging drunk driving. Second, when organizations give vigorous attention to drunk driving and its prosecution and prevention, the effort receives validation by the public, who in its turn perceives the organizational effort within a particular system of meaning.

Influence by Design. Symbols and systems of meaning can influence organizational culture in more deliberate ways as well. Organizations and programs will often incorporate external symbolism or systems of meaning from the environment to confer legitimacy on the organization and its behavior. A particular professional group might be made part of the organization, or a particular office might be established for legitimacy purposes. Throughout the 1970s the perception that banks made little effort to lend to minority customers, and perhaps practiced racism in their lending practices, became a prominent idea or way of understanding the public problem of minimal loans to minorities. This interpretation of bank lending practices and the political pressure behind it significantly influenced the three federal agencies charged with supervising banking activities. While under mandate to begin supervising the compliance of banks with consumer protection regulation, the Federal Deposit Insurance Corporation, Office of the Comptroller of the Currency, and Federal Reserve Board established offices of compliance and competed to hire banking supervisors specifically trained to monitor consumer protection activities of banks. Again, the system of meaning attached to the lending activities of banks provided meaning and incentive for the response of the three federal regulatory agencies to establish new regulatory offices and hire new professional staff. Resource commitments, training of compliance staff, and the priority given compliance by the regulatory agency all vary. As a result, groups interested in rigorous enforcement of consumer protection regulations view the three efforts with varied degrees of legitimacy, each using the system of meaning surrounding minority lending as a source of evaluation.[73]

Public managers can no doubt recognize a variety of such organizational responses to the institutional environment. Over the past twenty years virtually every agency in the federal government established policy analytic offices. The move could be viewed not only in response to congressional mandates for benefit–cost assessments of proposed rules and policies (part of the organization's formal institutional environment), but as conferring legitimacy upon agency decision making in a policymaking process increasingly embedded in the language of rationality and efficiency.[74] Today, public employees use the term *customers* to refer to members of the public, *performance* to refer to organizational outcomes, and *entrepreneurial* in reference to particularly innovative managers. The language resonates throughout organization reports, hearings before legislatures, and in daily management efforts. As the skeptics would understand it, adoption of this business language is an attempt to confer greater legitimacy on the work of government in a society with systems of meaning that elevate the work of business over the work of government. Whether these transfers actually improve organizational performance is another question. What is critical for the organization is the perception of legitimacy conferred upon the organization by participants in its environment.

Influence by Transplant. Finally, culture can be viewed as having its roots in the systems of meaning associated with professions or industries. Because people often come to organizations with a background or training in a particular profession or industry—each with its own system or approach to the work—their identity with the professional or industry group outside the organization can remain strong. Professors are members of an organization, a university or college, but they identify with professional organizations and broader communities outside of the campus, such as the American Political Science Association or the Association for Public Policy Analysis and Management. Each organization embraces at least one system of meaning that individuals can use to distinguish between a "professional" and an outsider. That system of meaning will also allow the individual to identify the rules for climbing the professional ladder and those for engagement between professionals and outsiders. An electrician or mechanic will bring to an organization a system of meaning ground in his or her education, experience, trade group, or labor union. An attorney will bring a particular set of ideas to the work of government that can differ significantly from that brought by an economist. Similarly, a public manager trained in a graduate business program might have a particular set of ideas about how government ought to be managed that is distinct from the set of ideas of a manager trained in a public management or public administration program. These ideas or approaches to work can significantly influence the way work is done in an organization and dominate the culture. Or, these carryovers might clash with other systems of meaning in the organization.[75]

The influence of external professions or industries can be particularly strong when an organization enjoys a high degree of autonomy from its immediate political environment. Expertise will provide an agency with power and autonomy if politicians depend upon that expertise and the agency is able to produce tangible results that are perceived by the public to be important or meaningful.[76] If organizations face competition in providing a particular type of expertise, or if the results of the organization's work are difficult to discern or controversial, the immediate political environment is likely to be active and intense in its scrutiny of the organization. This in turn might minimize the importance of a particular professional system of meaning (expertise) in the work of the organization.

High upon the list of organizations with autonomy is the Federal Reserve Board (the Fed).[77] Over the years government fiscal power—the spending and taxing power of the government—has become an ineffective tool for Congress and the president to manage the economy. As a result, politicians have come to rely heavily on the Fed to stabilize real incomes and prices by regulating the supply of money and credit. Despite continuous calls to make the Fed more accountable to the public and political overseers in its definition and execution of monetary policy, politicians do not want to be held responsible for an economic downturn connected to intervention with Fed policy. More importantly, they cannot agree on what, if anything, about Fed policy ought to change. One scholar finds, "The generations of complaints about the Fed reflect even more the extraordinary difficulty of reaching agreement . . . about economic problems when the political stakes are incalculably high."[78] The agency's skill in securing political support for its policies has fostered dependence upon the Fed's expertise to manage the money supply, as well as upon its interpretation of the status of the economy to determine whether Fed policy is working.[79] Within this setting, economic and banking expertise (systems of meaning) and a commitment to reasonable banking policy (a system of meaning shared throughout the banking industry and among other Western central banks) dominate the culture.[80]

The National Aeronautics and Space Administration (NASA) provides a contrast. The organization is no longer the principal source of scientific expertise for advancing the discovery and understanding of space and space technology and travel. Universities, private corporations, and other public organizations such as the Department of Defense compete for that expertise. Judging NASA's performance is also more complicated. When NASA put a man on the moon, the agency's expertise and success was beyond doubt. In the wake of the *Challenger* space shuttle tragedy in 1986, and numerous mishaps including lost space probes and faulty rockets, judging NASA's expertise has become more complex. Today, NASA's culture is less dominated by the academic expertise of various scientific disciplines in the lab and more focused on insuring responsiveness to political overseers in its restless political environment.[81]

INSIGHTS FOR THE PUBLIC MANAGER

Whether cultures react to environments, serving as safe passages through complexity and uncertainty, or absorb, select, or transplant the symbols and systems of meaning surrounding the work of the organization, the weighty impact of environment limits the influence a leader might have on the culture of an organization. As a representative of the fragmentation approach might point out, how can managers manage what is in constant and unpredictable fluctuation? Despite its grounding in the public sector, much of the research on culture offers practitioners in the public sector very little hope for diagnosing, let alone managing, the cultures of public organizations. There are, however, important insights that the public manager can take from both sides of the debate over managing culture.

Intertwined Influences:
Leadership and the Environment

Organizational leaders, the advocates argue, have the potential and responsibility to tend to culture. A leader is charged with understanding culture and insuring that the culture supports their vision and organizational goals. This might require maintenance of an existing culture, incremental changes in the culture, or wholesale reinvention of the culture. Whatever the culture–management task, *leadership* and culture are inseparable in the advocate world. For the skeptics, however, the *environment* and culture are inseparable. Culture on the inside of an organization, the skeptics argue, begins with or is deeply connected to the outside world.

Taking the leadership and environmental perspectives together, we could argue that public managers as leaders can be influential in the development and change of culture, but they must look for, understand, and work with the environmental factors that influence and interact with the culture they seek to manage. A public manager seeking to assess the environment and its impact on culture must think broadly and creatively about what constitutes the relevant context or environment for their organization. Beyond the formal rules, structures, and processes are norms, values, and customs; informal relations with organizations and constituencies; and public perceptions. Judgments about an agency's contribution, its value as a source of expertise, and responsiveness to its clientele, for example, may rest on informal parameters, but these parameters are nevertheless important for the ability of an agency to carry out its mission. Indeed, the key to the Federal Reserve Board's remarkable autonomy within government is the skill of its different leaders over time to build political and public support for its approach to managing the supply of money and its decisions in that regard.[82]

Viewing a manager as a leader able to direct and change an organization is not new to public management. For more than a century scholars have compared the leadership dimensions of public management to those in the private sector.[83] Reformers who call for a "new public management" or the reinvention of government view managers as entrepreneurial leaders with the capacity to create public value.[84] However, understanding the management of culture as one of the most important components of the job is a new dimension for public managers as leaders, as is the emphasis on the environment as a key component of that task.

Managing Culture Internally and Externally

Given the combined importance of leadership and environment, public managers might view the task of managing culture as an external as well as internal management effort. Management is actually a three-pronged task. Managers in the public sector must focus "*outward*, to the value of the organization's production, *upward*, toward the political definition of value, and *downward* and *inward*, to the organization's current performance."[85] The lessons of the advocates and skeptics lead us to a similar assessment. Managing a culture would seem to require attention to the environment and its changes, and an understanding of the ways in which the environment directly influences culture. Managers interested in changing culture must not only see these connections, but must also accept the challenge of trying to bring about changes in the environment to facilitate changes in culture. A top manager, for example, might work to improve communication between political overseers and the organization or provide better information on performance. Through speeches, press relations, and management actions, a system of meaning that constrains the perspective of an organization might be the target of a leader's efforts to alter public perceptions about a problem or policy. And managers might pay close attention to the ways employees perceive and serve the public, from the immediate clientele to the general population.

Persistence and Follow-through

The stubborn and overwhelming influence of the environment (in the view of the skeptics) and the difficult and never-ending job of managing culture (in the view of the advocates) point to another key lesson. Public managers must be persistent and follow through in trying to change and manage culture. Changing a culture has never been identified as an easy task, or even one that is ever complete. Rather, it is an ongoing effort, requiring the lion's share of a leader's attention and effort.

The message of persistence is important for the public manager who faces great resistance to change—in large part due to the environmental setting of her or his program—and often has little time to accomplish change. Any leader will face resistance to change by individuals, groups, and whole organizations.[86] Individuals might fear the unknown, find security in work habits, or resist change for reasons of self-interest or selective attention to, and retention of, the change efforts. Similarly, groups and divisions in an organization might resist perceived changes in power, or hesitate due to lack of trust. The organization might have resource limitations, fixed investments, or agreements with other organizations that are impediments to change.[87]

In public organizations, these factors are compounded by complex settings with a variety of political players that have stakes in the way organizations are structured and programs are implemented.[88] Members of the legislature or city council, their constituents and interest groups, programs that cross organizational and governmental boundaries, unions and professional groups with a stake in the way work is performed, all pose a source of resistance to change. For many public employees, the efforts of a leader to change an organization are viewed as the latest leadership fling. Career employees often simply wait until a leader's tenure is complete, and then resume with business as usual.[89]

It is precisely the short-term nature of many public management positions that limits opportunities for change—even change that is persistently pursued. If managers serve at the pleasure of a chief executive or city council, time is limited by the electoral cycle. Even when managers have more stable tenures, patience is not necessarily a virtue in the political world. Legislators, city council members, mayors, and governors all want results or change in rapid-fire fashion. The advice of the advocates, then, is crucial. A public manager interested in managing culture must focus intently on the dimensions of culture that require change, have a flexible plan, and pursue that plan relentlessly. The pursuit will no doubt be rocky, full of learning and adjustments, but the intensity of the process of change is crucial. If tenure is short and the effort tentative, then culture change will be negligible; if, on the other hand, the effort is relentless, then a leader may achieve a critical change in an organization's culture.

CONCLUSION

Public managers cannot ignore the arguments of either the advocates or the skeptics. Both groups have important lessons to offer the manager seeking to influence the culture of a public program. Part of a public manager's responsibilities as a leader is to seek out the connections between the environment and the existing program culture, and view the effort to change culture as both an inward and outward task. As the skeptics argue, cultures are deeply connected to the environment. To change the former, a leader must understand and work within the confines of the latter. As the advocates argue, changing a culture is tough, and the overwhelming influence of the environment on culture, combined with intricate internal influences upon culture, make any effort to change culture an ongoing battle. In the following chapter, we will use these lessons to develop the basis of a framework to understand and manage the cultures of public programs.

Notes

1. Robert Caro, *The Power Broker: Robert Moses and the Fall of New York* (New York: Vintage Books, 1975), 75.

2. Luther Gulick, "Notes on the Theory of Organization," in *Papers on the Science of Administration,* ed. L. Gulick and L. Urwick (New York: Institute of Public Administration, 1937), 1–45.

3. The committee's official title was the President's Committee on Administrative Management (1936–1937), chaired by Louis Brownlow. Charles Merriam (University of Chicago) and Luther Gulick (Columbia University, and founder of the Institute of Public Administration in New York City) were the other two members of the committee.

4. See, for example, the first and second Hoover commissions (1947–1949 and 1953–1955), both chaired by former president Herbert Hoover. Contrary to its mandate (to reduce the number of agencies established during World War II), the first commission focused on ways to strengthen the executive branch through reorganization of agencies according to function and to increase the capacity of the Executive Office of the President to manage government agencies. The second focused on ways to make government more effective and efficient by delimiting specific government functions and reducing government activities that competed with private sector efforts. The Advisory Council on Executive Reorganization (1971), appointed by President Richard Nixon and chaired by Roy Ash, advocated a significant restructuring of the executive branch. And in 1982 the President's Private Sector Survey on Cost Control, chaired by J. Peter Grace and established by President Ronald Reagan, focused on ways to make government run more like a private sector business. See Jay Shafritz and E. Russell, *Introducing Public Administration* (New York: Addison-Wesley, 1997), 115–119. See also Peri Arnold, *Making the Managerial Presidency: Comprehensive Reorganization Planning,* 1905–1996 (Lawrence: University Press of Kansas, 1998).

5. See, for example, Chester Barnard, *The Functions of the Executive* (Cambridge: Harvard University Press, 1938); and Philip Selznick, *Leadership in Administration* (Evanston, Ill.: Row, Peterson, 1957).

6. For excellent overviews of the culture literature see J. Steven Ott, *The Organizational Culture Perspective* (Pacific Grove, Calif.: Brooks/Cole, 1989); Harrison Trice and Janice Beyer, *The Cultures of Work Organizations* (Englewood Cliffs, N.J.: Prentice-Hall, 1993); Joanne Martin, *Cultures in Organizations: Three*

Perspectives (New York: Oxford University Press, 1992); and Linda Smircich, "Concepts of Culture and Organizational Analysis," *Administrative Science Quarterly* 28 (1983): 339–358.

7. John Kotter and James Heskett, *Corporate Culture and Performance* (New York: Free Press, 1992).

8. Terrence Deal and Allan A. Kennedy, *Corporate Cultures* (Reading, Mass.: Addison-Wesley, 1982); Deal and Kennedy, *The New Corporate Cultures* (Reading, Mass.: Perseus Books, 1999); and Rob Goffee and Gareth Jones, *The Character of a Corporation: How Your Company's Culture Can Make or Break Your Business* (New York: Harper Business, 1998).

9. Edgar H. Schein, *Organizational Culture and Leadership* (San Francisco: Jossey-Bass, 1985); Alan Wilkins and William G. Ouchi, "Efficient Cultures: Exploring the Relationship Between Culture and Organizational Performance," *Administrative Science Quarterly* 28 (1983): 468–481; and David Kreps, "Corporate Culture and Economic Theory," in *Perspectives on Positive Political Economy,* ed. J. Alt and K. Shepsle (Cambridge: Cambridge University Press, 1990).

10. Thomas Peters and Robert H. Waterman Jr., *In Search of Excellence* (New York: Harper and Row, 1982).

11. For a discussion of this connection, see Richard Scott, "Symbols and Organizations: From Barnard to the Institutionalists," in *Organization Theory: From Chester Barnard to the Present and Beyond,* ed. O. Williamson (New York: Oxford University Press, 1990), 44–45.

12. Barnard, Functions of the Executive, 279.

13. Ibid.

14. Peters and Waterman, *In Search of Excellence;* William Ouchi, *Theory Z: How American Business Can Meet the Japanese Challenge* (Reading, Mass.: Addison-Wesley, 1981); Deal and Kennedy, *Corporate Cultures;* and Richard Pascale and Anthony Athos, *The Art of Japanese Management* (New York: Simon and Schuster, 1981).

15. Deal and Kennedy, *The New Corporate Cultures;* Goffee and Jones, *The Character of a Corporation;* and Edgar Schein and Warren Bennis, *The Corporate Culture Survival Guide: Sense and Nonsense about Organizational Culture* (San Francisco: Jossey-Bass, 1999).

16. See Smircich, "Concepts of Culture," for a useful discussion of culture as an integrating factor.

17. Goffee and Jones, *The Character of a Corporation,* 15.

18. William Ouchi, "Markets, Bureaucracies and Clans," *Administrative Science Quarterly* 25 (1980): 125–141.

19. Ouchi, *Theory Z.*

20. Schein, *Organizational Culture and Leadership;* and Deal and Kennedy, *Corporate Cultures.*

21. John Andrews and Paul M. Hirsch, "Ambushes, Shootouts, and Knights of the Roundtable: The Language of Corporate Takeovers," in *Organizational Symbolism,* ed. L. Pondy, P. Frost, G. Morgan, and T. Dandridge (Greenwich, Conn.: JAI Press, 1983); Deal and Kennedy, *Corporate Cultures;* and Deal and Kennedy, *The New Corporate Cultures.*

22. Goffee and Jones, *The Character of a Corporation.*

23. Kreps, "Corporate Culture and Economic Theory"; and Gary Miller, *Managerial Dilemmas: The Political Economy of Hierarchy* (Cambridge: Cambridge University Press, 1992), 206–210.

24. Ouchi, *Theory Z.*

25. Peters and Waterman, *In Search of Excellence.*

26. Deal and Kennedy, *The New Corporate Cultures,* 3.

27. Richard Daft, *Organization Theory and Design* (St. Paul: West, 1995).

28. Peter Senge, *The Fifth Discipline: The Art and Practice of the Learning Organization* (New York: Doubleday/Currency, 1990); and Edgar Schein, *Organizational Culture and Leadership,* 2d ed. (San Francisco: Jossey-Bass, 1992). Schein is also the founder of *Reflections: The Journal of SoL* (Society for Organizational Learning), devoted entirely to the study and practice of generation, dissemination, and utilization of knowledge and skills in organizations.

29. Edgar Schein, "Organizational and Managerial Culture as a Facilitator or Inhibitor of Organizational Learning," SoL Working Paper, 10.004, May 14, 1994. Retrieved from the web on April 11, 2001, at http://www.sol-ne.org/res/wp/10004.html.

30. Goffee and Jones, *The Character of a Corporation.*

31. D. Nadler, "Organizational Frame Bending: Types of Change in the Complex Organization," in *Corporate Transformation: Revitalizing Organizations for a Competitive World,* ed. R. Kilmann and T. Covin (San Francisco: Jossey-Bass, 1988), 77.

32. Schein, *Organizational Culture and Leadership.*

33. Emerald Now: Management Learning into Practice, "Spotlight on Edgar Schein," March 2000. Retrieved from the web on November 25, 2001 at http://www.emeraldinsight.com/now/archive/mar2000/spotlight.htm.

34. Harrison Trice and Janice Beyer, *The Cultures of Work Organizations* (Englewood Cliffs, N.J.: Prentice-Hall, 1993), 264–268; and Trice and Beyer, "Cultural Leadership in Organizations," *Organization Science* 2 (March–April 1991): 149–169. The authors argue that the primary challenge for a charismatic leader is to attract followers and unite them. If the leader's vision and philosophy are to become the basis of culture, he or she must also find ways to "routinize" charisma so that his or her "radical vision" and mission can come to fruition.

35. Donald Kettl, *Leadership at the Fed* (New Haven: Yale University Press, 1986); and Anne Khademian, *The SEC and Capital Market Regulation: The Politics of Expertise* (Pittsburgh: University of Pittsburgh Press, 1992).

36. Khademian, *The SEC and Capital Market Regulation,* 23–45.

37. Trice and Beyer, *The Cultures of Work Organizations,* 254–298.

38. Ibid.; see also Schein, *Organizational Culture and Leadership,* both editions.

39. Hal Rainey, "Building an Effective Organizational Culture," in *Handbook of Public Administration,* ed. J. Perry (San Francisco: Jossey-Bass, 1996), 151–166.

40. Kotter and Heskett, *Corporate Culture and Performance;* Alan Wilkins, *Developing Corporate Character: How to Successfully Change an Organization Without Destroying It* (San Francisco: Jossey-Bass, 1989); and Schein, *Organizational Culture and Leadership,* 2d ed.

41. Goffee and Jones, *The Character of a Corporation.*

42. George Huber and William Glick, "Sources and Forms of Organizational Change," in *Organizational Change and Redesign: Ideas and Insights for Improving*

Performance, ed. G. Huber and W. Glick (New York: Oxford University Press, 1993), 11.

43. Khademian, *The SEC and Capital Market Regulation,* 152–182.

44. Rainey, "Building an Effective Organizational Culture."

45. Deal and Kennedy, *The New Corporate Cultures.*

46. Edgar Schein, "Organizational Culture," *American Psychologist* 45, no. 2 (1990): 115.

47. Trice and Beyer, *The Cultures of Work Organizations,* 406–408.

48. Khademian, *The SEC and Capital Market Regulation.*

49. James Q. Wilson, *Bureaucracy: What Government Agencies Do and Why They Do It* (New York: Basic Books, 1989); Herbert Kaufman, *The Forest Ranger: A Study in Administrative Behavior* (Washington, D.C.: Resources for the Future, 1960); and Kaufman, *The Administrative Behavior of Federal Bureau Chiefs* (Washington, D.C.: Brookings, 1981).

50. Kaufman, *The Administrative Behavior of Federal Bureau Chiefs,* 118.

51. Wilson, *Bureaucracy,* 90–110.

52. See, however, Trice and Beyer's very thoughtful discussion of the environment in *The Cultures of Work Organizations,* 299–354.

53. Martin, *Cultures in Organizations,* 113, emphasis in the original.

54. Selznick, *Leadership in Administration.*

55. Martha Feldman, *Order Without Design: Information Processing and Policy Making* (Palo Alto: Stanford University Press, 1989).

56. Selznick, *Leadership in Administration,* 137.

57. Ibid., 40.

58. Ibid.

59. Donald Warwick, *A Theory of Public Bureaucracy: Politics, Personality and Organization in the State Department* (Cambridge: Harvard University Press, 1975).

60. Ibid., 161.

61. See Martha Derthick's study of the Social Security Administration's efforts to implement two new programs that required assumptions and approaches distinct from traditional management efforts. The study is also an excellent example of the overwhelming influence of a political environment on the way work is done in a government organization. Derthick, *Agency Under Stress: The Social Security Administration in American Government* (Washington, D.C.: Brookings, 1990).

62. Carolyn Ban, *How Do Public Managers Manage? Bureaucratic Constraints, Organizational Culture, and the Potential for Reform* (San Francisco: Jossey-Bass, 1995).

63. See, for example, Martha Feldman's study of policy analysis in the Department of Energy in *Order Without Design.* See also Martha Feldman, "The Meanings of Ambiguity: Learning From Stories and Metaphors," in *Reframing Organizational Culture,* ed. P. Frost, L. Moore, M. Louis, C. Lundberg, and J. Martin (Newbury Park, Calif.: Sage, 1991), 145–156.

64. Martin, *Cultures in Organizations.*

65. Ibid., 159.

66. Ibid., 141–152.

67. Scott, "Symbols and Organizations." In addition to systems of meaning, an "institutional" perspective offers a variety of ways to understand and examine the relevant environment for an organization, such as interorganizational connections, and

the ways in which organizations in a similar field influence each other. Different types of organizations are also associated with different thicknesses of environmental institutionalization. See Paul DiMaggio, "Structural Analysis of Organizational Fields: A Blockmodel Approach," in *Research in Organizational Behavior*, Vol.8, ed. Barry Staw and L. L. Cummings (Greenwich, Conn.: JAI Press, 1986), 335–370; and Richard Scott and John W. Meyer, "The Organization of Societal Sectors," in *Organizational Environments: Ritual and Rationality*, ed. John Meyer and Richard Scott (Beverly Hills, Calif.: Sage, 1983).

68. W. Edwards Deming, *Out of Crisis* (Cambridge: MIT Press, 1986).

69. For a discussion of the differences between quantitative and qualitative cultures, see Virginia Hill Ingersoll and Guy Adams, *The Tacit Organization* (Greenwich, Conn.: JAI Press, 1992), 40.

70. Ralph Hummel, *A Critique of Life in the Modern Organization*, 4th ed. (New York: St. Martin's, 1994), 80.

71. Ingersoll and Adams, *The Tacit Organization*, 40–41.

72. Joseph Gusfield, *The Culture of Public Problems: Drinking-Driving and the Symbolic Order* (Chicago: University of Chicago Press, 1981).

73. Anne Khademian, *Checking on Banks: Autonomy and Accountability in Three Federal Agencies* (Washington, D.C.: Brookings, 1996), 145–165.

74. Deborah Stone, *Policy Paradox: The Art of Political Decision Making* (New York: W. W. Norton, 1997).

75. Martin, *Cultures in Organizations*, 85.

76. Francis Rourke, *Bureaucracy, Politics and Public Policy*, 3d ed. (Boston: Little Brown, 1984).

77. This does not mean that the Fed is free from influence or oversight. A large literature examines Federal Reserve Board activities to determine the agency's responsiveness, or lack of responsiveness to elected officials. See, for example, Thomas Havrilesky, *The Pressures on American Monetary Policy* (Boston: Kluwer Academic Publishers, 1993); John Woolley, "Partisan Manipulation of the Economy: Another Look at Monetary Policy with Moving Regression," *Journal of Politics* 50 (1988): 335–360; and Nathaniel Beck, "Presidential Influence on the Federal Reserve in the 1970s," *American Journal of Political Science* 26 (1982): 415–445. As Donald Kettl writes, "the keystone of the Fed's power . . . is not so much its legal independence as its success in winning political support for its decision." See Kettl, *Leadership at the Fed*, 11.

78. Kettl, *Leadership at the Fed*, 212.

79. Ibid., 11.

80. Khademian, *Checking on Banks*.

81. Barbara Romzek and Melvin Dubnick, "Accountability in the Public Sector: Lessons from the Challenger Tragedy," *Public Administration Review* 47 (1987): 227–238.

82. Kettl, *Leadership at the Fed*.

83. Woodrow Wilson, "The Study of Administration," *Political Science Quarterly* 2 (1887): 197–222. For an interesting comparison of a private sector leadership and public management leadership, see Robert Behn, "Branch Ricky as a Public Manager: Fulfilling the Eight Responsibilities of Public Management," *Journal of Public Administration Research and Theory* 7, no. 1 (1997): 1–33.

84. Mark Moore, *Creating Public Value: Strategic Management in Government,* (Cambridge: Harvard University Press, 1995); and Robert Reich, ed., *The Power of Public Ideas* (Cambridge: Harvard University Press, 1988). The leader as entrepreneur, however, is controversial. See Larry Terry, *Leadership of Public Bureaucracies: The Administrator as Conservator* (Thousand Oaks, Calif.: Sage, 1995); and Peter Aucoin, *The New Public Management: Canada in Comparative Perspective* (Montreal: IRPP, 1995).

85. Moore, *Creating Public Value,* 73, emphasis in the original.

86. Trice and Beyer, *The Cultures of Work Organizations,* 402.

87. Ibid.

88. Terry Moe, "The Politics of Structural Choice," in *Can the Government Govern?* ed. J. Chubb and P. Peterson (Washington, D.C.: Brookings, 1989).

89. Warwick, *A Theory of Public Bureaucracy.*

A Cultural Roots
Framework

BETWEEN 1990 AND 1995 the East St. Louis Action Research Project (ESLARP) was transformed from an annual appropriation that funded research and project designs conducted by University of Illinois faculty to an intricate, productive partnership between neighborhood organizations, East St. Louis residents, university faculty and students, and numerous government and nonprofit agencies. At the core of the transformation was a change in culture. Efforts by Professor Kenneth Reardon, lead faculty for ESLARP from 1990 to 2000, changed the way the work of ESLARP was done by changing the way the work was defined, examined, and shared between East St. Louis residents and members of the university. Reardon established a commitment to shared responsibility and a commitment to continuous evaluation for strengthening the partnership.[1]

James Lee Witt's leadership of the Federal Emergency Management Agency (FEMA) produced a phenomenal transformation in the preparedness and responsiveness of the agency to victims of natural and nonnatural disasters because he was able to effect fundamental change in the way the job got done. Before Witt's tenure, FEMA was suffocating from lack of internal and external communication. The agency was lost in the haze of a complicated mission, stooped from a top-heavy bureaucracy, despised by the public it was meant to serve, and vilified by its congressional overseers. When Witt came on board he worked to change FEMA's culture by establishing basic commitments to open communication and to meeting the needs of FEMA's customers.[2] Within five years FEMA had won the appreciation and praise of its clientele and elected officials.

A partnership between the New Haven Department of Police Service and the Yale University Child Studies Center significantly altered the way police and mental health clinicians encounter, counsel, and treat children exposed to violence. The Child Development–Community Policing (CD–CP) mental health partnership empowered police officers on the scene of violence to begin addressing the needs of affected children by providing the officers with mental health education and weekly interaction with Yale University mental health specialists. At the same time, clinicians expanded their understanding of children exposed to violence by working in partnership with police and other community organizations and responding with immediate and community-based treatment as an alternative to clinical settings. The program, begun in 1990 under the leadership of New Haven police chief Nicholas Pastore and physicians in the Child Studies Center at Yale, was grounded in Pastore's efforts to alter a well-established, insular police culture increasingly steeped in militaristic techniques to one committed to understanding the community and engaging in professional partnerships such as the partnership with Yale. Both commitments drove the work of police and mental health clinicians in the CD–CP mental health partnership and contributed to a 22 percent reduction in crime during Pastore's tenure.[3]

Such dramatic changes in culture are obvious to the observer. But just how do culture changes take place? What, if anything, did these and other public managers do to change the basic commitments of public programs and, as a result, change the priorities, performance, and public perceptions of the programs they lead? In this chapter we will develop a framework for understanding and managing the cultures of public programs. The framework is built upon two basic premises. First, cultures evolve from efforts to conduct a public task with specific resources and skills in complex environments. The gradual integration of task, resources, and environment produces commitments, or rules for how the job gets done, in public programs. These three elements—task, resources, environment—are the "roots" of culture.

Second, public managers as leaders don't manage culture per se. Rather, they influence and help shape commitments by managing the process of integration, or the way the roots of culture weave together to influence the resulting commitments (see Figure 3.1). Managing the integration of a task with particular resources in a complex environment is an inward and outward effort for the public manager—he or she must focus his or her efforts both inside the program and outside toward the environment within which the program operates. The effort must also be relentless. Culture change does not take place or stay in place unless the nature and understanding of the task, the resources and personnel involved, and key dimensions of the environment are continuously managed.

While many government reformers have noted the importance of culture change for improving government performance, the nitty-gritty details of how change might be accomplished in public programs has never been addressed. In this chapter we will use our framework as a rudimentary map with which to begin our investigation into what these details may be. The framework, built as it is from the conclusions drawn from the wealth of research on culture discussed in Chapter 2, provides a relatively sturdy investigative vehicle with which to traverse these uncharted waters. The examples presented here also offer some suggestions for thinking about ways in which culture change might take place. In short, the

Figure 3.1 Managing the Roots of Culture

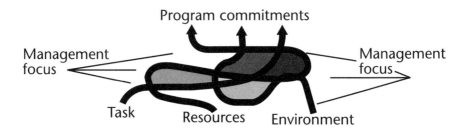

information in this chapter serves as a starting point for future, more focused investigations of culture in public programs, its role in performance, and its manageability.

THE PRODUCTION OF CULTURE

What are the factors that form and shape the culture of a public program? Stepping back from the world of public policy for a moment, we can look at the simple example of a farmer growing a crop of corn for harvest to illustrate some of the forces at work. The farmer's task has specific dimensions: the preparation of the soil; the planting of the seeds; tending to the seeds and eventually the stalks and ears of corn; and harvesting, selling, and delivering the corn to a buyer. His task requires specific resources and skills as well. Seeds, fertilizer, a plow, a tractor, and planting and harvesting equipment are essential. Just as essential, the farmer must have both the skill and the knowledge to accurately gauge the timing of the planting; to utilize the most productive and efficient forms of fertilizer, planting, and irrigation; to operate and maintain the equipment; and to manage the financial and business dimensions of the project. He may need additional help at harvest time depending upon the size of the crop and the speed required to harvest it. Finally, the planting and eventually the harvesting of the corn are conducted within a complex environment. Each step in the process and each decision are made within a legal framework of environmental regulations and public policies aimed at protecting or encouraging farming. Weather conditions change unpredictably; organized farm groups provide support and advice; other farmers compete in the production of corn in the same region and around the globe; and the systems of distribution, production, and sales function within a complex web of economic interests.

The farmer's annual effort to plant and harvest corn, which depends on a mix of skills and resources in a complex and changing environment, will gradually produce commitments, or informal rules that guide the way in which the farmer does his work. For example, a commitment that bases the timing of the various tasks of farming on rules of thumb about the weather could take hold. Similarly, a commitment based upon the relationship of the task to the environment and markets could evolve. Given a set of environmental conditions, and the expectations for selling the corn and to whom, the farmer might commit to mechanizing every dimension of the task, going organic, or trying to maximize the efficiency and speed of his operation without great attention to pollution or some crop loss. Finally, the relationship between the farmer and the eventual buyers and distributors of the corn could be another possible basis for the development of a commitment that would play a crucial role in determining the way the task was done. The farmer might opt to trust his various business partners, not trust them, or trust but verify.

This type of integration of the task, the resources, and the environment provides the roots of culture in public programs as well. First, a manager is responsible for a particular task or tasks. The U.S. Mint prints and coins money. State-based Friends of the Court enforce court orders for visitation and child support. Prisons confine and sometimes rehabilitate convicted criminals. State and county social service agencies enroll eligible residents for supplemental income, provide services from health care to child support and job training, and facilitate contact with a variety of other government agencies and nonprofit organizations. And libraries maintain and circulate books and a variety of media for residents of a particular geographical area. Each task is unique in its combination of skills, implementation systems, and final product.

Second, the manager must pursue the task with a particular set of resources, including personnel with varied training, socialization, and learned methods of approaching the task. Some tasks involve unionized workforces. Others draw upon nonunionized professionals, from health care, the law, and education to public affairs, science, economics, and engineering. Financial resources in public sector programs are typically tight. For state, local, and nonprofit organizations participating in public programs, in particular, funding is complicated by a diversity of sources, including the federal government, general funding, user fees, or private foundation support.

There are also the rare public tasks that are conducted with, if not an abundance, at least plentiful resources. Some public programs generate income through fees or services that the organization is permitted to keep. The Federal Reserve Board (Fed) in Washington, D.C., which determines the nation's monetary policy, assesses the twelve regionally located Federal Reserve Banks for its operating expenses. The Fed also earns income from data processing services, subscription fees for its publications, and assistance provided to other federal agencies. Still other agencies benefit from a public and political perception that the task for which they are responsible is of great importance and hence operate with plentiful budgets. Before its first mission to the moon, for example, NASA was flush with resources and political support—both the public and the federal government were eager to beat the Soviet Union to the moon.[4] These variations on personnel and resources matter for the way work is done within an organization. Alterations in resources and personnel can significantly impact organizational commitments.

Finally, managers must pursue public tasks with particular resources and within the expectations, constraints, and legacies of complex environments. Partisan politics, political ambition, and reelection campaigns continuously collide with public program management.[5] More formally and predictably, government programs operate within constant waves of new initiatives and reform, some aimed explicitly at the structure, design, and management of programs and some aimed more generally at the conduct of government affairs. Each manager works within mandated personnel and procurement systems, budget processes, and cycles of oversight and reporting to political superiors. The work of the program is received and understood in distinct ways by the immediate consumers of the program and by the broader public that observes the program. A history follows the program, with a legacy that weighs heavily on the way tasks are interpreted, the ways employees communicate with clientele, and the ways political overseers communicate with and relate to the program.

Like the evolution of commitments that define the planting, tending, harvesting, and sale of corn by a farmer, the integration of a public task with particular resources and within a complex environment eventually produces commitments that define the way the job gets done in a public program. Commitments are manifest in a variety of ways: the physical space of a government program, specific language and patterns of communication, symbols, common understandings, frames of reference, relationships within and outside the program, and the basic organization and execution of work.

Participants in a program learn that these commitments can provide a guide to understanding the program itself and their work within it. How should they define the task, and what role do they play in bringing that task to fruition? Commitments help participants interpret the relationship of the program to the public served. Do they view the public as customers or as a needy clientele? Are they experts providing the public with the benefit of their expertise? And commitments can provide motivation and perhaps a sense of identity. Commitments need not be functional in the context of program objectives or form a coherent, integrated culture. Indeed, if corporate cultures are ground in past success, as many advocates argue, public sector cultures can evolve as a means to survive, and program survival does not necessarily equate with coherence and program performance.

But just as the farmer has influence over the way resources are used, the extent of his own knowledge and training and that of any employees, and his relationship with farming groups, buyers, and distributors, a public manager can influence the way task, resources, and environment are integrated to produce commitments.

MANAGING CULTURAL ROOTS: SIX STRATEGIES FOR CHANGE

There are six strategies aimed at understanding and changing the culture of public programs. Each one builds from the following basic point: If managers want to change culture, they must focus on the roots of culture and manage the way in which task, resources, and environment are integrated. The strategies draw upon the lessons of the advocates and skeptics presented in Chapter 2 and the examples of the public sector managers who were able to change the culture of their public programs presented at the beginning of this chapter. Box 3.1 presents a summary of the six strategies.

Strategies 1 and 2: Identify the commitments that form the existing culture and identify the connections between the roots of culture and commitments. A public manager must understand the existing culture of a public program before trying to bring about change. The techniques used by social scientists conducting field research offer managers a way to tackle this task. In a landmark study of congressional "home styles," or the way members of Congress present themselves to their districts, one scholar describes his research method as "soaking and poking."[6] Field research involves a great deal of hanging around, observing people, and soaking up data about the phenomenon under study. Soaking up data requires that one step back and detach oneself from the action, dialogue, and events in order to see a broader picture and identify patterns. To poke around, however, requires engagement. The researcher must probe, ask questions, check other sources, and ask more questions to discern the veracity of patterns, frameworks, and systems of thinking and organizing that emerge from her or his field research.

A public manager seeking to change program culture must both "soak and poke" to discern the existing commitments that define the way work is done and the connections between commitments and the roots of program culture. He or she must step back from the daily activities and routines of the program to discern patterns in communication and behavior and methods of interaction within and without the program. By stepping back the public manager may also be able to identify symbols, stories, and dress that might offer insight into the commitments of a program. A public manager must also probe, testing the relevance of patterns that emerge and examining the broader context within which the program exists. What is the primary task of the program and how do participants define and pursue that task? What are the key resources involved in conducting the task? What types of background, skills, and training produce effective personnel? What are the primary environmental factors that draw the attention of participants or that have historically been critical to the work of the program? The

---

Box 3.1 Six Strategies to Understand and Change Culture

1. Identify the commitments that form the existing culture.
2. Identify the connections between the roots of culture and commitments.
3. Think about what needs to change and articulate the change.
4. Understand the management of cultural roots as an inward, outward, and shared responsibility.
5. Relentlessly practice and demonstrate the desired changes in culture.
6. Capitalize on incremental change and institutionalize it.

---

manager must probe to find connections between these factors and the identified commitments.

Strategy 3: Think about what needs to change and articulate the change. Successful managers do not establish a clear strategic plan and follow it to the letter. Rather, they have a clear vision of where they want to go and use practice and experimentation to get there. This is management by "groping along."[7] To grope is to experiment to find out what works, but experimentation with a clear vision.[8] A manager seeking to change program culture will develop a clear idea of what needs to change, articulate it, and grope along to find a way to accomplish that change. It may be clear that a particular commitment inhibits innovation or prevents a program from focusing on the needs of clients. The manager could then focus on changing these commitments to bring about better client service and creative ways of accomplishing that service. Replacing the old with the new, however, will require constant articulation of what the new commitment or commitments ought to be, and groping along to get there—experimenting with the integration of task, resources, and environment.

Strategy 4: Understand the management of cultural roots as an inward, outward, and shared responsibility. A leader will work to bring about changes by understanding the effort as an inward, outward, and shared responsibility. Leaders trying to manage the roots of culture will focus inward toward the definition of the task and the application of resources and skills. They will also look outward toward the environment for elements significant to the development of program commitments. The manager must work with elements of the task, resources, and environment to find a process of integration that fits with his or her vision of program performance. If a manager pursues an alternative definition or understanding of the task of a public program, and experiments with alternative applications of resources and personnel, there will most likely be consequences in the program environment. Political supporters and opponents, program clientele, organized interest groups, other organizations, and even other governments could take notice and possibly object if they have interests in maintaining particular definitions of the task and particular applications of resources. If new commitments are to evolve, the manager must work with people, groups, and other organizations to facilitate, or at least not to inhibit, the changes.

Managing the integration of task, resources, and environment is also a shared responsibility. A single leader might initiate the effort, but change in the culture of a public program involves the broad participation of program employees and managers or leaders in related offices, organizations, or programs. Depending upon the manager and the changes she or he wants to make, a change in culture might also require the participation or cooperation of program clientele and other members of the public. For example, the changes might entail a reconstruction of the way clientele and members of the public perceive, experience, and evaluate the program, requiring broad participation in public forums, surveys, and other forms of feedback.

Strategy 5: Relentlessly practice and demonstrate the desired changes in culture. Public managers must be relentless in their efforts to manage the integration of task, resources, and environment to bring about changes in culture. As such, managing the integration of cultural roots becomes an ever present dimension of management responsibilities. Central to this responsibility are continuous evaluations of the way the job gets done and a willingness to critically review efforts and make changes if doing so will facilitate program performance.

Strategy 6: Capitalize on incremental change and institutionalize it. Finally, changing a culture is a radically difficult task, requiring continuous applications of energy. Even with a clear focus, careful analysis, and devotion to the work of the program, not all dimensions of the roots of culture are manageable. When there is recognizable change, even the most incremental, finding ways to institutionalize the change can preserve it and foster more of the same.

In the following sections we will see how these six strategies were put into action in the cases of three public sector managers working to manage culture.

IDENTIFYING COMMITMENTS

Often a single, clear commitment captures the essence of an organizational culture. That commitment might be deeply embedded in the mandate and work of the program, such as the defining commitment of the Federal Deposit Insurance Corporation (FDIC), the agency responsible for managing the government-sponsored insurance fund for bank depositors. The FDIC's central commitment is to protect the fund, which drives the ways the agency conducts supervision of banks, resolves banks that have failed, and trains new employees.[9] Protecting the fund provides employees with a sense of identity—why they do what they do—and a means to maintain the relative autonomy of the agency. As long as the bank insurance fund is solvent, political overseers take a minimal interest in the details of agency activities and leave the supervision of banks and the resolution of bank failures to the professionals in the FDIC. In other programs the central commitment might be less connected to the task at hand, but rather represent a means to cope with the complexity and fog surrounding a public program mired in public and political scrutiny.

When James Lee Witt assumed responsibility for FEMA in 1993 the agency was a conglomeration of programs with minimal communication or coordination between them. In 1979 President Jimmy Carter had signed an executive order that pulled together under one roof five programs from different executive branch departments to create an agency responsible for managing civil defense and other emergency management programs. These combined programs (or directorates, as they were called) were to organize and assist relief efforts in the event of a nuclear attack on the United States or natural disasters such as earthquakes, fires, floods, or hurricanes. The programs varied in their responsibilities, ranging from the development of civil defense plans to the support of state and local governments in emergency preparation, training of firefighters, public education, and the administration of national warning and communication systems.[10] While congressional intent was to create a single agency focused on disaster preparation and relief, the capacity of FEMA to act in concert was severely limited by a lack of coordination between programs. In a report issued by the National Academy of Public Administration (NAPA) in 1993, an interviewee described the agency as "a check-writing agency, an intelligence agency, a social service agency and insurance agency, with a fire administration thrown in."[11] Witt offered a similar analysis on his arrival:

> [Initially] FEMA's mission was focused primarily on natural disasters. In the 1980s, the priority was preparing for a nuclear attack. By the time I got there, the Cold War was over, natural disasters were still striking, and nobody had a clear sense of what they were supposed to do.[12]

Witt saw dedication on the part of individuals in the agency to accomplish the work of FEMA, but the commitment was to the work in individual directorates, and communication between the programs was minimal. "People in different directorates wouldn't share information. . . . and information is power," Witt explained.[13] He attributed the lack of coordination, communication, and cooperation between directorates to a lack of leadership:

> Every baseball fan knows that when you've got a great lineup that's working hard, but losing games, you don't blame the players. You blame management. The manager is responsible for marshalling their skills towards a clearer goal of winning that game. And that's what FEMA was like when I arrived. We had terrific people. They weren't producing because they weren't being led. Very dedicated people.[14]

Witt began his tenure with FEMA by trying to open communication with and between employees and programs. "[F]or a long time," Witt noted, "it was difficult to get them to even talk to me, because there was a mentality there that they were not used to, that openness."[15] Without communication between programs within FEMA, communication with FEMA's external partners—governors, state disaster relief offices, nonprofit organizations and coalitions providing disaster relief—as well as with its political overseers and the public suffered too.[16] Witt's efforts to re-create FEMA involved tremendous structural and procedural change. But he conducted these efforts within a broader attempt to blast open communication within the agency itself and between the agency and its partners and the public it serves. As we shall see, he also sought to pry open and coordinate individual programs by focusing employee attention on the task of serving FEMA customers—members of the public, state and local emergency management personnel, governors and other elected officials, and even FEMA employees themselves.

For Kenneth Reardon, the new faculty director of the Urban Extension and Minority Access Project (UEMAP) in 1990, a commitment to detached academic expertise inhibited a working partnership between the University of Illinois and residents of East St. Louis. As discussed in Chapter 1, faculty in the School of Architecture and in the Departments of Landscape Architecture and Urban and Regional Planning designed approximately three dozen projects between 1987 and 1990 intended to revitalize East Saint Louis, Illinois. Only one project—a manufactured housing factory—made it from the drawing board to implementation, and that was largely thanks to the efforts of state representative Wyvetter Younge.[17] The university, in plain terms, was not extending itself to the community. The residents of East Saint Louis did not have as much access as the title of the program suggested. Professors, not residents, were understood to have the expertise to address the problems and find solutions. Academic expertise determined the organization of UEMAP and the structure of its work. Faculty practiced what critics referred to as windshield sociology, examining the city and its problems through the window of a car. Research and project developments were conducted primarily on campus, with accountability for finished projects and funding directed to the individual chairmen of the three departments.

The process of stepping back and identifying the existing commitments that define a culture is akin to "soaking and poking." How do participants talk about the work of the program? How do they communicate with each other, with program clientele, and with others outside of the program? How is the program organized? Who or what ideas dominate the way the task is interpreted? For James Lee Witt, managing by walking around FEMA, hanging out with its employees, and establishing an open-door policy helped give him a clear picture of the communication problems—and the consequent low morale—dominating the organization. His first day on the job, Witt began by standing in the lobby and greeting each FEMA employee in the morning. He shook hands, introduced himself, and listened to anyone who would talk to begin establishing the basis for future communication. The sour expressions, hunched backs, grumbles, and hunkered-down body language revealed a great deal about the strain of working under intense political and public scrutiny without the resources or leadership to change or coordinate programs within the agency. Witt also gathered information about the agency while walking around, stopping at each desk, talking about the job, floating ideas for doing things differently, and meeting with anyone who wanted to talk in person or by phone every Tuesday morning.[18] Perhaps most critically, Witt's experience as state emergency management director of Arkansas gave him an understanding of FEMA's communication problems, particularly with its state disaster relief partners, and its poor coordination between programs.[19] Commitments to minimal communication, and even the withholding of information, as well as to the work of individual programs clearly inhibited the potential of FEMA to coordinate and provide disaster relief with its numerous partners.

When Nicholas Pastore began his tenure in 1990 as chief of police with the New Haven police department, he had a clear sense of the culture driving traditional police behavior. He knew that it was a culture that inhibited the kind of partnerships he sought to build with the community—partnerships such as the Child Development–Community Policing mental health partnership. It was, as Pastore described it, a "pronounced culture of power" driven by the commitment to respond with force after a crisis or crime occurred.[20] Pastore's leadership in New Haven was dedicated to uprooting this militaristic culture and replacing it with a community-based approach to policing geared to service to the entire community. This would entail building partnerships with the community and other professionals to mitigate and prevent crime and to address the challenges of New Haven as a community. The CD–CP partnership was a natural extension of these efforts. It grew from the conviction that understanding and working with the community was a first step to meet the mental health needs of children exposed to violence and perhaps improve the ability of the community to prevent violence in the first place.

Traditional police culture and training of officers stood in the way of such a partnership. Officer involvement with children exposed to violence drew from standard police procedure. When a child or parent is a suspect or a reluctant witness to a crime, "police officers—especially in the midst of a crisis—might not think about children's emotional needs."[21] Traditional mental health care for children also stood in the way of a professional partnership. A basic commitment to treat children in clinical settings by mental health professionals limited exposure of clinicians to the community setting where violence occurred. Pastore and Dr. Donald Cohen of the Yale University Child Studies Center began to forge a partnership built around a simple observation: Treatment of a child exposed to vi-

Table 3.1 Old and New Program Commitments

Program	Old Commitments	New Commitments
ESLARP	Academic expertise	Shared responsibility; continuous evaluation
FEMA	Focus on the work of individual programs; minimal communication	Open communication; dedication to the customer
CD–CP Mental Health Partnership	Professional responsibility "after the fact;" clinical-based treatment	Understand the community; professional partnerships

olence begins when police arrive on the scene, giving police officers an opportunity and responsibility to play a role in the child's development.

As part of his efforts to blend the work of these two professional groups, Chief Pastore focused on shifting power and resources to provide his police officers with the skills, expertise, and clout necessary to engage and work on a par with mental health clinicians in addressing the needs of children in New Haven. A description of the program offered by the New Haven Department of Police Service pinpoints the effort to reorient police officers through training and education:

> Fundamentally, the program attempts to reorient police officers in their interactions with children in order to optimize the psychological roles which they can play as providers of a sense of security, positive authority, and models for children.[22]

The managers of FEMA, ESLARP, and the CD–CP Mental Health Partnership identified the dominant program commitments that inhibited the capacity, as they and many others saw it, of their respective programs to perform. They were then able to articulate and pursue alternative commitments (see Table 3.1). But before the transition could take place, these managers had to identify and work with the connections between the roots of the existing culture and the commitments.

IDENTIFYING THE CONNECTIONS BETWEEN THE ROOTS OF CULTURE AND COMMITMENTS

Public managers don't directly manage culture. They manage the integration of a task with resources and environment. In other words, their primary focus is on the roots of culture. The older and more established a program, the deeper the roots—the more ingrained the definition and understanding of the task, the more established and accepted the resources and personnel associated with the task, and the more familiar the environment. Identifying connections between program commitments and the (often deep) roots of culture is essential if change is desired. As we will see in our discussion of ESLARP, the commitment to academic expertise had very deep roots in the surrounding environment—the university setting, political circumstances, and public perceptions of urban poverty.

The Expectations, Constraints, and Legacies of Complex Environments

Every public program has a complex environment. It has a history, a formal political environment and possible competitors, clientele, professional and trade organizations, and a variety of organized interests that may float in and out of the environment depending upon the issues or challenges facing a program at any given time. And public perceptions of the program are embedded in systems of meaning that help shape public understanding of the importance of the program and how well it is performing.

Given the mix of public and political expectations, conflict, constituents, and legacies, some managers simply have "impossible jobs in public management."[23] When faced with such situations, managers may develop coping strategies to navigate the "multiple, conflicting, and unrealistic concerns and constituencies," but they will "never master or control [the impossible job]."[24] By any measure, the expectations, conflict, constituencies, and legacies surrounding UEMAP made the transformation from a detached program based upon academic expertise to a working partnership based upon participatory research an impossible job in public management. The program was initiated following testimony by then University of Illinois president Stanley O. Ikenberry before the Illinois House of Representatives's Standing Committee on Education Appropriations. Chairwoman Wyvetter Younge challenged Ikenberry to demonstrate the university's commitment to the needs of cities like East St. Louis. UEMAP was established in 1987 with an annual grant of $100,000 in university funds to support faculty and student research projects aimed at improving environmental, social, and economic problems in the city.[25]

From the state legislature, Representative Younge provided public support for the UEMAP projects, but the broader political context of UEMAP was more complicated and presented a roadblock to completion of the projects, as well as to a more participatory partnership between the university and city residents. Most critically, the East St. Louis city government was unable and often unwilling to work to secure funding for the projects. In 1990 the city government was preoccupied with its own financial crisis—a crisis so bad the city was ordered by a judge to transfer the title to City Hall and 240 city-owned waterfront acres to satisfy the claim of an individual harmed in the city jail.[26] The city's financial stress was alleviated to some degree in 1991 with $30 million in long-term financing from the state legislature, but acceptance of the money came with state oversight and constraints on the city's budget.[27] More importantly, a Democratic political machine that controlled most of the jobs in a city with very few private employers stifled change that might have spotlighted the city government's inadequacies or taken away sources of power from the political machine. In fact, as the program transitioned from UEMAP to ESLARP, refusal on the part of residents and community organizations to broker requests for services through the party organization resulted in critical delays of service:

> [The resident's] refusal to use favored architects, planners, lawyers and insurance agents for neighborhood improvement projects, regardless of their qualifications, has not been appreciated by local party officials. While municipal officials voiced support for ESLARP's projects, they often failed to approve necessary plans or to provide modest amounts of project funds in a timely manner. Such delays, on occasion, have jeopardized the success of several of the community's self-help efforts.[28]

Just as critical to the evolution of ESLARP was the university setting. Early in the program the commitment to academic expertise was reinforced by traditional tenure reviews of faculty that rewarded publications rather than outreach. This would be a primary barrier to the evolution of ESLARP. Young faculty members were discouraged from participating in the program if it was at the expense of a more extensive publication record. Publication pressures prompted the partial withdrawal of two Urban Planning faculty members from the project in the late 1990s and strained ESLARP's continuing efforts to focus on building the capacity of local organizations. While publication and tenure pressures limited the interest of junior faculty, more senior faculty often already had developed research agendas and institutional responsibilities that limited the time they had to work three hours away from campus in a community service capacity.[29] Within the university setting, in other words, the legitimacy of faculty participation rested with a detached approach to research—publication was honored, but not necessarily participatory research.[30]

Within the university, UEMAP, and eventually ESLARP, was also constrained by the concern that other communities would seek assistance from the University of Illinois—an anxiety soon realized when the university received requests for ESLARP-like efforts from several urban areas in Illinois.[31] While the university publicly promoted the eventual successes of ESLARP and provided $100,000 (and eventually $250,000) annually, long-term financial stability required an endowment for recurrent funding. In the words of Professor Reardon, this didn't happen during his tenure because ESLARP was in competition with other priorities for endowment money.[32] And finally, internal political con-

straints emerged from competition between the University Cooperative Extension Service and ESLARP. The Extension Service defined its own mission as outreach, and the ESLARP model of participatory research was in direct contradic-
tion with the Extension's centralized model of outreach. Between the two,
Extension was the more established program within the university hierarchy,
which gave it more clout in arguing against university support of the participatory approach. In other words, the Extension posed another political hurdle in
the ESLARP environment.[33]

A program environment also consists of perceptions of clientele—in this case,
residents of East St. Louis. Reardon argued that among the many white students
and faculty participating in ESLARP, as well as in the broader public, "unexam-
ined attitudes towards African Americans influenced by many negative stereotypes" could cause students and faculty to "hold East St. Louis residents solely responsible" for the problems of the city. The failure to consider "structural factors
such as technological change and corporate disinvestment that undermined the
city's economy" not only influenced perceptions of the problems in East St. Louis,
but also caused deep resentment among residents who worked hard to maintain
their family, homes, and community.[34] At the core of this system of meaning used
to understand urban decay and poverty was what Reardon called the "boot strap"
rule: "We've always believed that those who worked harder, ran faster, succeeded."
But, Reardon argued, "When you dig deeply into East St. Louis, you see people
who have worked every bit as hard at more difficult jobs, and look what they
have. . . . It puts into question those rules."[35] Perceptions of residents were also influenced more vaguely by the belief in academic expertise over resident participation as the preferred approach to the problems of inner cities. This understanding
did less to define the clientele than to heighten the relevance of academic studies
and program designs as a means to address urban decline.

Finally, the UEMAP, and eventually ESLARP, environment consisted of professional academic affiliations that influenced the way the job was done and con-
ditioned Reardon's efforts to alter the way work would be done. For example, the
Housing and Community Development Act of 1992 authorized the federal Department of Housing and Urban Development (HUD) to establish a grant program for institutions of higher education to establish and operate Community
Outreach Partnership Centers (COPCs). As HUD's web site describes the program, grantees are encouraged to "apply research to urban problems, coordinate
outreach efforts with neighborhood groups and residents, act as a local information exchange, galvanize support for neighborhood revitalization, develop public
service projects and instructional programs, and collaborate with other partnership centers."[36] Altogether, the University of Illinois received more than
$500,000 in 1995 and 1997 for its COPC efforts connected to ESLARP.[37] But,
as Reardon perceived it, COPCs also created constraints to building partnerships
patterned after ESLARP. It was, he said, a movement for reforming and revitaliz-

ing inner cities that concentrated the control of the planning process in the hands of professional planners.[38]

Like most public programs, ESLARP's environment was complex. A city facing political and financial crisis; a university with priorities, concerns, and expectations built upon traditional academic practices; public perceptions of poverty and of the residents of East St. Louis; and broader, professional connections all stood in the way of a commitment to participatory research, or shared responsibility. Prior to Reardon's tenure, this complex environment helped foster a commitment to academic expertise and a more detached approach. As we will see later in this chapter, Reardon directly engaged this complex environment to bring about new program commitments.

The Nature of the Task

In addition to the environment of a public program, the nature of the task is a root of program culture. A public manager trying to identify the connections between program commitments and the roots of culture must also understand the ways in which the task—what the program does—influences program commitments. The task placed before the University of Illinois and its UEMAP project was immense: to find ways to stabilize, revitalize, and enhance the quality of life in the city of East St. Louis. Previous government-funded programs were unable to address, let alone stabilize or slow, a long list of problems plaguing the city. Decades of out-migration by residents and businesses left little if any tax base to address the basic social needs of East St. Louis—collecting trash, policing the streets, educating children. A city government run by a political machine had little incentive to be responsive to the concerns and demands of residents. But residents were tired and skeptical of yet another program that seemed to benefit only university participants and not the city itself. And although Representative Younge carried a great deal of clout with the university, threatening to hold up annual funding if a commitment to urban renewal was not forthcoming, even her remarkable influence was not sufficient to establish a working partnership toward urban renewal. The task seemed an impossible one unless interpreted and approached as a series of research projects designed by faculty who in turn left development and implementation questions to the politicians. The impossible job of *implementation* was simply defined out of the task under UEMAP.

In the case of FEMA, no clear definition of the task existed. Communication between programs lagged before the appointment of James Lee Witt, largely because the nature of FEMA's task was not clear—to itself, its partners, the public, or its political overseers. At a broad level, FEMA's mandate split the agency between emergency management programs focused on preparation for and recovery from natural disasters and civil defense (essentially, preparation and planning for a possible nuclear attack). In the 1980s, with the cold war still raging, civil defense initiatives consumed most of the agency's budget. As a result, the resources and expertise needed to coordinate and manage programs targeting natural disasters were severely neglected.[39] More narrowly, it was not clear to FEMA officials how the agency was to exercise its influence with the states and localities, as well as with other government agencies, to coordinate emergency programs. A matter of FEMA management style complicated the question of authority. Much of the work on civil defense was secretive, with only the agency and the defense community privy to its particulars. The coordination of emergency management programs, however, required outreach and interagency coordination.[40] The two styles were at odds, and the definition of FEMA's primary task was left hanging in the balance.

Without a clear definition of the task, FEMA employees muddled through. The agency's incompetence—characterized by poor communication and lack of focus—in handling relief efforts following Hurricane Hugo in 1989 prompted Sen. Ernest Hollings, D-S.C., to refer to FEMA employees as "the sorriest bunch of jackasses I've ever seen in my life."[41] And Rep. Norman Mineta, D-Calif., complained that FEMA "could screw up a two-car parade" following its performance in the 1989 Loma Prieta earthquake.[42] An agency culture committed to the work of individual programs and minimal, if any, information-sharing clearly did not facilitate the ability of the agency to prepare for, and aid recovery from, natural disasters. The commitments that evolved before Witt arrived were perhaps a means to avoid the fragmented and confusing nature of FEMA's overall task.

The task of building a partnership between the New Haven Department of Police Service and the Yale University Child Study Center was daunting. Two elaborate and entrenched professional systems—police work and mental health counseling—required adjustment. Boundaries that defined the work of police and the work of mental health professionals needed to be blurred and woven together at key points of intervention to meet the needs of children exposed to violence in an immediate, community-based, and flexible manner. Police officers required alternative training and education to better understand the mental health needs of children on the scene of violence, and mental health professionals needed to be educated about police work and learn new ways to counsel outside of the clinic, either on the spot or in the home. Communication between the systems and individual officers and counselors had to be built. The task required nothing short of overcoming legendary bureaucratic turf, entrenched professional standards of behavior, and, in particular, a deficit of trust between the community and police.[43]

Focusing specifically on policing, Nicholas Pastore connected the existing police commitment to response after the fact (after a crime was committed) to a traditional understanding of the police officer's role to defend the status quo. To build a program like the CD–CP partnership would require a new understanding of the police officer's role (or task) as an active professional participant in the community. Police officers needed to be engaged and trusted members of the community, as well as educated about the needs of children exposed to violence. Uprooting the traditional task definition and seeking to replace it with Pastore's view of community engagement was an essential element in building a program committed to a professional partnership between police and Yale University mental health clinicians.

Public managers must examine the ways in which participants in a program define and understand the task of the program, and the way they themselves understand it. By contrasting and connecting these understandings to existing commitments, managers will be able to identify connections between the application of resources and personnel and the existing commitments.

Resources and Personnel

The training and background of personnel involved in a public problem also play a critical role in determining program commitments. Professionals have great power not only in determining the way the job gets done in public programs, but also in the interpretation of the problem the program is intended to address.[44] A definitive study of professions and the public sector argued that professionals seek autonomy and dominance in their decision making in a public program or organization. A professional group wants to exercise independent expertise and use a public organization or program as a base or foundation to protect and promote the relevance of that expertise.[45]

Academics trained to conduct research and teach within specific disciplines exercise tremendous autonomy in the work that they do at public universities. Members of the University of Illinois faculty conducting the work of UEMAP played an important role in developing the way work was done between 1987 and 1990. Finding solutions for the problems of East St. Louis was approached as a research project, with the goal of producing objective, empirical research and conceptually sound designs. The professional framework for academic pursuits provides minimal encouragement for, if not outright discouragement of, academic engagement in bringing about the changes or recommendations that the research suggests. Most critically, universities reward faculty with tenure based upon their records of publication. Direct engagement with governments, communities, or groups to put the ideas to work is time consuming and takes the scholar away from research. The effort also places the scholar in the position of taking sides, which threatens objectivity with the appearance of having an agenda. This in turn threatens the autonomy of the profession itself. The public policy academic community has long struggled to establish itself as an objective source of information that can be applied by policy makers to the public problems of the day.[46] Directly engaging the political process to bring research to fruition cuts across the grain of these efforts.

In addition to faculty expertise, the other primary resource for UEMAP was funding. An annual $100,000 allocation from the university was split between three programs: Architecture ($50,000), Landscape Architecture ($25,000), and Urban and Regional Planning ($25,000). Between 1987 and 1990 spending was not coordinated between the three departments, and faculty reported to the chairs of their respective departments.

In short, resources and personnel did little to encourage a direct partnership with the residents of East St. Louis and a lot to foster the commitment to academic expertise. Similarly, prior to 1990, the training and experience of police officers and mental health professionals in New Haven did little to encourage a partnership for addressing the needs of children affected by violence. Police officers were trained to respond rapidly to crime, arriving at scenes of violent crime after it occurred. "At best, traditional police strategies and tactics can provide children and families a sense of security and safety through rapid, authoritative, and effective responses at times of difficulty. All too often, however, children's contacts with police officers arouse fewer comforting feelings and more negative ones."[47] Mental health professionals are traditionally trained to address children's mental health needs in clinical settings, also after the fact. There was minimal capacity within the mental health services system of New Haven, and among mental health professionals, to tailor treatment and timing of treatment to the individual needs of children. Chief Pastore and Dr. Cohen in the Yale Child Study Center faced the challenge of bringing these two professional systems and the individuals who peopled them together. They were able to do so with the benefit of Yale University resources. Yale mental health professionals trained individual police officers in child development and made themselves available to respond immediately to the needs of children exposed to violence. The police department, for its part, assigned officers to single neighborhoods so that the officers could get to know the residents of the neighborhood and become familiar with their problems. At the same time, residents could get to know the officers in their neighborhoods, building trust between residents and the New Haven police.[48]

Prior to 1993, FEMA resources and personnel did little to facilitate communication within the agency and with its outside partners, or to prompt coordination between FEMA directorates. There was little support for a coordinated approach to all disasters, natural or man-made, with FEMA as the lead federal agency. Resources and skilled personnel were heavily tilted toward the more secretive portion of FEMA's mission, preparation for a nuclear attack. Between 1982 and 1992 FEMA spent twelve times as much money preparing for a nuclear disaster than preparing for natural disasters.[49] Of the agency's five major directorates during this period, four played a role in civil defense.[50] Given this lopsided distribution, it should not be surprising that the agency was severely criticized in reports issued by the General Accounting Office (GAO) for its limited capacity and expertise to oversee management of earthquake preparation, hurricane preparation, and even the oversight of basic procurement efforts for the agency.[51] As one of the three roots of culture, the distribution of resources and skills facilitated the inclination to isolate and hold on to information, and to focus people on the work of individual programs rather than prompt a more open, combined approach to managing disaster relief. As James Lee Witt put it, "Nobody woke up in the morning thinking how can we do a better job of preventing disasters today? They woke up thinking well what does my program need today?" [52]

Understanding the ways the roots of culture—resources and personnel, task, and environment—connect to existing program commitments provides managers with a map of program culture, and a focus for change. In the words of Chief Pastore, "You analyze the culture, and do your best to redact what's working. . . . What are the successes and failures, and what are the cause and effects?" [53]

DETERMINING AND ARTICULATING CHANGE

With a mental map of the cultural roots in their respective programs—an understanding of the successes and failures, causes and effects—managers of ESLARP, the CD–CP partnership, and FEMA began the process of changing culture by specifying and continuously articulating what needed to change, and why. Kenneth Reardon's initial vision for the work of UEMAP had two sources: The expectations and concerns of residents of East St. Louis and the social theory of participatory research. After Reardon assumed responsibility for UEMAP he drove three hours from Urbana–Champaign to East St. Louis to find out if the program was working. Fifty or more interviews with community leaders and residents revealed the answer: a resounding "no." Residents, according to Reardon, were sick of grand designs and abstract conceptualizations. Many of the residents interviewed had participated extensively with university-based consultants through the numerous public programs aimed at improving the economic and social status of urban centers.[54] Many of these efforts, they claimed, focused on the central business district or the waterfront of the city, leaving residential neighborhoods little consideration. Residents told Reardon that these efforts "often ignored the rich reservoir of knowledge and insights local residents and business people possessed regarding community dynamics."[55]

Reardon and several of his colleagues from the Department of Urban and Regional Planning decided they wanted to use the $25,000 allocated to their department (out of $100,000 split between three departments) to develop a long-term partnership with any East St. Louis residents who would work with them. The Emerson Park Development Corporation, representing the neighborhood of Emerson Park, agreed to commit to the partnership, on several conditions. Any partnership, the residents argued, would be contingent upon an approach that gave the community control over the research agenda, included residents in every step of the process, placed greater emphasis on implementation of planning efforts, and was committed to helping local organizations raise funds.

The theory of participatory research provided guidelines for trying to bring about shared responsibility. The theory requires faculty to approach community planning at the grassroots level, relying on residents to "identify the issues to be examined, participate in the collection of field data, and collaborate in the analysis of this information."[56] The top-down approach to planning that guided early work in UEMAP would be abandoned. Reardon and other faculty pursued the participatory research approach with residents of Emerson Park to develop a comprehensive plan to stabilize the neighborhood and its economy. When these and later efforts met resistance from the city and county governments, participants introduced a second component of the project—direct action organizing.[57] Residents and university participants mobilized to influence the city government. A plan to turn five trash-filled lots into a toddlers' playground in the Winstanley/Industry Park neighborhood, for example, required resident mobilization targeting recalcitrant local and county officials responsible for tax delinquent properties in the city. Resident delegations were established to meet with these officials, and a postcard campaign encouraging action targeted the officials. Letters to the editor of the *East St. Louis Monitor* from local leaders created a high level of visibility for resident efforts, as did the recruitment of over two hundred residents to attend meetings on the topic.[58] The success of direct action organizing was the impetus for changing the name of the program from UEMAP to the East St. Louis Action Research Project, and direct action organizing took its place as another critical responsibility that would be shared among participants.

Reardon began by identifying the elements of UEMAP culture that prevented it from effecting a real working partnership between the university and East St. Louis residents. Having done so, he gained a clear picture of how he could change the way work was done. Specifically, he listened to the complaints of the residents and then sought to meet their expectations of what an effective partnership should be, using the theory of participatory research to do so. He spoke continually with fellow faculty, students, and residents of what participatory research involved and how it could work for the program. Reardon often told the story, both verbally and in writing, of how the program evolved to include direct action organizing as a key component of shared responsibility, and later to include community education. His reiteration of the value of participatory research and the twin strategies of direct action organizing and community education conveys the ways the commitment to shared responsibility evolved and highlights its importance to the program. The name change alone was an important signal of the program's newfound commitment to partnership and real change for the residents of East St. Louis.

James Lee Witt came to FEMA already armed with a basic understanding of what needed to change and why. His interactions with the agency as director of emergency management in the state of Arkansas had prepared him for what to expect at FEMA. Nevertheless, the degree to which coordination, communication, and a central focus for the agency were problematic was surprising. As Witt recalled, "I was amazed at what I found in the agency itself."[59] He began his tenure with a three-day retreat with a facilitator for all senior managers. He kicked off the retreat with a statement about what he wanted to accomplish at FEMA that included a list of his goals and priorities. Managers were then asked to break up into teams and draw up their own management plans, priorities, and goals (they could add or subtract from his own list) and define a new mission for the agency. Witt then left the meeting, returning three days later. According to Witt, "It worked wonderfully." Over the course of just one retreat, he was able to forge new lines of communication by placing the managers of the individual directorates together on working teams and giving them the authority to think broadly and creatively about how FEMA should operate in the 1990s.

Throughout his tenure, Witt was very open in his efforts to communicate. "[A]s leader and a manager, I feel like we have to be open," Witt argued. "[W]e have to be concerned, and we have to talk to people and we have to share, and that was very difficult at first."[60] Witt pursued this effort to open communication on a daily basis and in a variety of ways. In addition to his open-door policy and Tuesday morning meetings, he established a director's weekly letter and a weekly publication called the "Rumor Mill"—answers to all the rumors phoned into an agency "hot line" each week.[61] It was within this context of more open communication that FEMA employees and Witt developed a clear mission for FEMA:

> Reduce the loss of life and property and protect our institutions from all hazards by leading and supporting the Nation in a comprehensive, risk-based emergency management program of mitigation, preparedness, response, and recovery.[62]

Within this context Witt also promoted a clear customer focus: "A partnership of people helping people."[63] Rather than focus on the needs of individual programs, Witt wanted FEMA employees to focus on the needs of their customers— the American public, particularly victims of disaster; federal, state, and local partners in disaster relief; members of Congress; and even FEMA employees themselves. As one FEMA supervisor noted following the 1994 earthquake in Los Angeles:

> Witt gave employees this sense that they needed to do whatever it took, within the law, of course, to get out there and get help to people as quickly as possible, bureaucracy be damned. . . . There was this sense that we could sort out the ad-

ministrative details later, if necessary, so long as people were getting the help they needed now. [64]

Helping FEMA's customers meant communicating with all of them about ways to prevent, mitigate, and deal with disasters and ways to use FEMA resources and expertise to facilitate those efforts. Witt was persistent in conveying the importance of good communication to both help the nation and build partnerships. "Communicate your message, communicate your message, communicate your message. I can't say it enough," Witt told a leadership forum.[65]

In order to create a partnership with the Yale Child Study Center, Nicholas Pastore needed to attend to a broader concern: developing a police force whose professional identity focused on understanding and serving the residents of New Haven. Rather than continuing to emphasize the power of officers to carry and use weapons, wear bulletproof vests, and make arrests, Pastore articulated first the need to understand and respect the community that the officers served. "One of my first mission statements," Pastore noted, "was 'Be Nice.'"[66] His officers, Pastore believed, needed to understand and respect the varied neighborhoods and communities served by the New Haven Department of Police. This message was communicated through a sign outside his office that read: "Police others as you would have them police you."[67] This message of understanding and respect was continuously communicated in various forums, from the routine training of officers to the implementation of conferences and seminars focused on officers and members of the community. Topics included "Police and the Black Family," "Cops and Kids," "Dealing with Lesbian and Gay Violence," and "Domestic Violence: Rethinking Police and Community Response." A cable television show cohosted twice weekly by police officers and community members also provided a forum for articulating the message of community service and community partnerships.[68] This push to communicate the importance of a police force focused on community service was an essential component of Pastore's efforts to build a commitment to a professional partnership with Yale's Child Study Center. As Pastore understood it, his officers needed to know and respect the New Haven community in order to develop the capacity to work as professional partners in a program focused on meeting the mental health needs of children exposed to violence.

Pastore communicated what needed to change, and why, in his own daily activities. He was a constant presence in the city, often walking the streets without a jacket and without a gun. "I wanted to show that the streets are safe, and show them [officers] the way."[69] The action was a bold one in a city where violence was spinning out of control and mistrust of the police was endemic. Pastore's efforts to connect with residents were not only attempts to shift the perceptions held by police officers, but to begin to mend the divide between the community and the police. Before police officers could become community-based professionals working in partnership with mental health clinicians, or any other professional organization, they needed to develop a rapport with the community. Finding community-based treatment options for children exposed to violence and working to mitigate and even prevent violence and its consequences required knowing a neighborhood and its families, as well as knowing the organizations and treatment options available. "We had to seek the help of the community," Pastore noted. "I would go to meetings, social events, even break bread. . . . We call it getting down with the people."[70]

In his daily communication with officers, Pastore used language that changed the point of reference for police efforts, orienting them toward the changes Pastore sought. Referring to a case that helped launch the CD–CP mental health partnership, Pastore described an incident in a home where one man stabbed another to death over the affections of a woman. The police detective on the scene walked the chief through the maze of yellow crime scene tape and gave him the rundown on the facts of the case. Everything seemed to be all wrapped up when Pastore happened to peer around the corner in the home to the next room where six children sat on a sofa with a woman who was trying to comfort two of them. The children had witnessed the crime. Pastore responded, "Our job is not done. How many victims? One or seven?"[71] By asking how many victims, Pastore provided for his officers a different frame of reference from which to view their role at the crime scene. And by telling the story of the children who had witnessed the violence, he began to communicate the need for the police to develop the capacity to respond to such situations.

Determining what needs to change and articulating those changes is an essential part of the effort to manage the integration of cultural roots. If managers want to change how the job gets done, they must understand the commitments driving the work of the program and how those commitments might need to change. Articulating those changes helps participants to see the task, the resources, and the skills they bring to the table, and the environment in which they work, differently.

MANAGING CULTURAL ROOTS: INWARD, OUTWARD, AND SHARED RESPONSIBILITY

In order to bring articulated changes to fruition, managers must directly engage the roots of culture. This means the management effort must be pursued as an inward, outward, and shared responsibility. First, managers must focus inside the public program on the application of resources and personnel and the understanding of the public program task. Second, managers must engage with the outside environment, making changes or offering support as necessary. Third, managers must understand that the responsibility of managing the roots of culture and bringing about changes in the integration of program roots is one they share with a broad range of participants both inside and outside of the program.

Inward Efforts

To manage inward is to focus primarily on the personnel and resources within a program. Key to building a commitment to a professional partnership between the New Haven Department of Police and the mental health clinicians of Yale University was the hiring and training of police personnel. Chief Pastore had a plan not only for developing personnel prepared to work in the CD–CP mental health partnership but to develop the capacity to conduct community policing in New Haven. He described his efforts to find an approach for change: "I had to take many courses and I learned about Theory A and Theory B, and every theory had a protracted time table. . . . Police chiefs don't live that long. So I came up with my own—ventilation."[72] Pastore focused on members of the force who stood in the way of a new approach to policing and community partnerships:

> The system made them scoundrels. They were trained not to be nice people. . . . So we ventilated, bringing in new thinking people to select, train and educate differently. . . . We ventilated those in charge of selecting and recruiting and assigned them to patrol. . . . After a few months they soon left when they saw things would be less adventurous.[73]

To pursue this "less adventurous" approach to policing, Pastore hired a new training director with no police experience but with a Ph.D. in theatre and education. "If we humanize the selection and training of police officers," Pastore argued, "it checks their [officers'] trained reflex to pull out a gun first."[74] The emphasis in academy training shifted to sensitivity training, or understanding the special populations in New Haven and the low quality of life for many New Haven residents. These populations included the mentally ill, homeless people, people living with HIV and AIDS, drug addicts, and many single women trying to raise children on very limited incomes. Officers were required to live in a homeless shelter, meet with HIV-infected people at a hospice, and spend time with teenagers and gang members. They were also required to write a thesis about these experiences. In addition, trainees participated in staged conflicts designed to help them improve their communication and mediation skills.[75]

The training focused on building a professional partnership with mental health clinicians was an extension of the training techniques and information used to establish a community-based police force. Blending the resources of the New Haven Police Department and the Yale Child Study Center, a series of seminars and fellowships were instituted for training patrol officers, officers in supervisory positions, and mental health clinicians. Senior officers served as fellows in the Yale Child Study Center, where they were educated on the developmental and mental health concerns of children, as well as to the techniques and approaches needed to empower patrol officers to conduct intervention at the scene of violence. Mental health clinicians similarly served with police as fellows, learning about policing techniques and working with officers to develop strategies for collaborative intervention to meet the needs of children. A ten-week seminar was developed to prepare patrol officers for positive interventions with children and families, and weekly case conferences provided the opportunity for officers and clinicians to follow and discuss particularly difficult cases and ways to improve the treatment.[76]

Pastore's efforts to change the way policing was done in New Haven targeted the selection and training of personnel. The new paradigm in training—focused on understanding the community—provided a bridge to professional partnerships such as the CD–CP mental health partnership.

Ken Reardon's efforts to change the way work was done in ESLARP also began with changes in personnel and resources. Most critically, he made the effort to bring residents into the program as equal partners in the participatory research process. As described earlier, Reardon interviewed residents to identify their concerns about a partnership and to find out what their expectations were and what conditions needed to be met before an effective partnership could begin to take shape. The participatory research framework provided the initial map for negotiating the delicate partnership between the residents of the Emerson Park neighborhood and university participants. But perhaps most dramatically the switch to participatory research altered the pool of resources (expertise and personnel) available to the program. The experiences of a resident living in East St. Louis became as valuable a resource in the planning process as the academic expertise of university faculty. Referring to the planning, design, building, and operation of a farmers market, Carol Perry, president of the Winstanley/Industrial Park Neighborhood Organization in 1994, noted, "They talked about, what do *you* want, and I think that was the most important thing. They did not say, what *we* can do."[77]

Once a partnership was established, residents participated in recommending and pushing for internal changes in the operations of ESLARP. Prior to 1995, the ESLARP approach to the partnership was guided by the commitments to participatory research and direct action organizing. In Reardon's words, at that point "we were so proud of ourselves, we thought we would receive the Nobel Peace Prize. But then the residents called us down. . . . They said the approach was colonial, racist, and sexist. . . . We had our bell rung. It was a shock!"[78] Specifically, the residents were pointing to inequities in the training needed to effectively participate. Students received fifteen hours of training each week through university courses while residents received none. "Such practices," argued one resident, "reduce our role to the flea on the tail of the dog."[79] The Neighborhood College was established in East St. Louis to offer interested residents courses each semester that would help them participate meaningfully in community improvement, including courses on community-based crime prevention, state and local governance, economics, multiculturalism, and working on the Internet. The Neighborhood College was an important third commitment in the ESLARP framework: a commitment to popular education. The establishment of the Neighborhood College also represented another key commitment: Continuous critical evaluation of the program to ensure a quality partnership was essential to maintaining the support of all participants in the project.

Reardon and his faculty colleagues also altered the mix of personnel and resources by working to establish the Neighborhood Technical Assistance Center (NTAC) and hiring a professional planner, architect, community organizer, and grant writing expert. In August 1996 NTAC established itself as the university's physical presence in East St. Louis, able to handle 30 to 50 percent of the projects proposed by the East St. Louis Community Action Network (ESLCAN), the formal voice for community organizations through which proposed plans and suggestions needed to pass. NTAC was funded by the East St. Louis Community Development Block Grant Operations Corp., the U.S. Department of Housing and Urban Development, and the University of Illinois at Urbana–Champaign. The office provided technical and organizational assistance to community organizations ranging from research, mapping, and analysis of data to grant writing, nonprofit management, and volunteer recruitment.[80] Perhaps the most critical job of NTAC was that of community organizer. NTAC functioned as the lead organizer for ESLCAN and the facilitator of direct action organizing. Officially, the community organizer is called an "extension educator," but direct action organizing is a critical element in maintaining the partnership toward urban renewal—a fact that matters for the way ESLARP negotiates its environment.

An executive committee was eventually established within the university staffed by long-time ESLARP faculty. Any project that was very preliminary, or that required more physical effort, labor, design, or detail than the NTAC could handle, was bumped up to the University of Illinois campus. The faculty executive committee decided which projects could be done by student volunteers through courses, which by a studio course, and which by ESLARP graduate students. It could also decide if additional faculty needed to be hired for a specific task or special problem.

The implementation of undergraduate courses and graduate studio courses focused on the work of ESLARP brought hundreds of students into the participatory research project over the course of Reardon's tenure. Many graduate students completed master's theses, and one dissertation was conducted on an ESLARP project (at one time there were thirty-nine ESLARP graduate students). The incorporation of students into the project served three purposes. First, students participating in a course or studio related to ESLARP learned ways to connect the expertise of the university to the needs of communities. Participatory research is a theory that must be practiced to be understood. Through the students, Reardon and other like-minded academics were promoting a vision of partnership to future generations. Second, the studios and classes provided a forum for training future community development professionals in the methods of participatory research that emphasized the importance of cross-disciplinary efforts. Mike Andrejasich, a participating faculty member from the School of Architecture, described the efforts to build a farmers market in the Winstanley/Industrial neighborhood as an "interdisciplinary undertaking." Students participating in the effort learned "how the other disciplines use their particular expertise to attack the problem." The students begin to recognize, he argued, that "no one discipline alone is up to solving something as large and complex." [81] Finally, the students provided an invaluable source of energy and labor for the immense projects tackled by ESLARP. A single class did a project on illegally dumped trash in which they surveyed the garbage, developed a strategy for clean-up, established a budget, and so forth. The community organizer brought people together to document the trash, photograph it, and sample it to find out where the garbage came from. The organizer then pulled all the participants together, helped develop a strategy for attacking the problem, staffed the public hearings, and organized demonstrations and rallies and a candlelight march. [82]

James Lee Witt focused his early internal efforts on changing the way FEMA employees worked together and how they understood the primary tasks of FEMA. "FEMA," Witt recalls, "was an agency that had a lot of little agencies internally. They did not work together. They did not coordinate together. There was a tremendous waste of time and talent." [83] Witt referred to the organizational tendencies as "stovepiping." Each directorate had a distinctive understanding of the tasks charged to FEMA. Building upon the work of the retreat, a new mission focused on response and recovery, preparedness, and mitigation gave the "little agencies" a clear, common focus and guided an extensive reorganization of the agency into five new directorates, each a component of the new "all-hazards" approach. FEMA, in other words, would build its capacity to manage and coordinate emergency programs for any type of disaster. Three of the five new directorates reflected the wording in the new all-hazards mission: Response and Recovery; Mitigation; and Preparedness, Training, and Exercises. The other two directorates represented dimensions of FEMA's mandate to manage programs dealing with flooding and fire. The Federal Insurance Administration was responsible for managing the flood insurance program focused on helping people recover from floods and to prevent future loss (through mitigation and preparedness) due to flooding. The U.S. Fire Administration was charged with training firefighters to combat fires and educate people about fire prevention. [84]

In addition to his focus on the definition of the task and the organization of the agency to tackle the task, Witt targeted communication technology within the agency. He described the initial information systems as "alphabetic soup." Each program had its own system, and "none of the systems would talk to each other. . . . The problem was that . . . nobody wanted to give up their systems. But people didn't have the benefit of knowing what the person next door was even doing. Because they could not talk to each other."[85] A new information system began to change that situation. The changes realigned communication within the agency and worked to improve the ways in which FEMA communicated with its external partners by connecting FEMA offices to each other and connecting FEMA with the states.

Witt also focused on altering the perspectives of his employees. Beginning at the top of the agency, he initiated a complete shake-up of his senior managers. More than 80 percent of FEMA's Senior Executive Service (SES) staff was switched to new positions to promote new ideas and bring alternative experiences to the posts created in the reorganization and to reduce the personal stakes individual managers might have in changing the work of the agency.[86] Witt relied heavily on the initiative and ideas of top managers he regarded as both committed to and capable of making change happen at FEMA. In his view, all they needed was the opportunity. With some initial guidance by Witt, SES managers led the reorganization and mission building efforts at the retreat. Later, they changed jobs. The job changes no doubt facilitated efforts to alter the employee focus from what was a strict adherence to the rules and processes of individual programs to one aimed at finding any legal means possible to service FEMA's many customers.

The transition to a customer service orientation was also facilitated by training courses that all FEMA employees were expected to take and a series of awards given to FEMA employees for thoughtful and creative efforts. In 1993 Witt initiated a customer satisfaction survey to be sent to victims of disasters who were served by FEMA. The survey results were less than glowing. Some surveys came back with attached pages of comments. Witt and FEMA employees used the survey information to build a customer training program for all FEMA employees.[87] When someone did an outstanding job, Witt created a series of awards to recognize the effort, including an "on the spot" award that a supervisor could give instantaneously to any employee. An example of terrific customer service, or efforts that contributed to FEMA's overall performance, could be rewarded with one day or an entire week of vacation time. Cash awards and in some cases recognition by the director at a special ceremony were also part of the system intended to focus employees on taking the initiative for finding ways to improve customer service and make FEMA a vital, helpful public agency.[88]

The inward efforts of Nicholas Pastore, Ken Reardon, and James Lee Witt to manage the understanding of the program task and the application of resources and personnel were paralleled by their outward efforts to manage the third dimension of cultural roots—the environment.

Outward Efforts

To manage outward is to focus on the environment of a public program to try to maintain, change, or perhaps subtly influence the impact of groups, organizations, public perceptions, politicians, and program clientele on the way the job is done. ESLARP's direct action organizing made the effort to manage the environment an explicit part of its operations. When not a single proposal out of 96 included in the Emerson Park Neighborhood Revitalization Plan received external support from city, county, state, or federal governments, participants believed the line between research and direct action needed to be breached. When the Winstanley/Industry Park Neighborhood Improvement Plan was completed in the early 1990s, residents went to work to secure funding. They attended city council and county board meetings, circulated petitions, wrote letters to the editor, met with elected officials, and eventually secured $950,000 to implement their plans.[89]

As discussed above, such direct action efforts within the city of East St. Louis became a central premise of the ESLARP program, but efforts to navigate and change the environment were focused on the university as well. Reardon and his colleagues were pursuing an approach to planning that was viewed as contrary to the traditional pedagogical approach of the university, as well as to the relationship of the university to the community. "We have faculty complaining of the same students we had in ESLARP, that they were impossible to teach," Reardon stated in an interview. But the same students, he continued, were so excited to be part of ESLARP. "It's all substance, context, process. . . . In 1995 I supervised more theses than the entire department. It wasn't because I was such a great teacher [but because of the intense interest in ESLARP.]"[90] The ESLARP process, he argued, was a way to bring young people into planning, but a very different approach to planning than that based upon detached professional expertise.

As the lead faculty of ESLARP, Reardon was persistent in writing and speaking about the institutional constraints imposed by the university on the ESLARP effort. His primary complaints centered around the need for permanent, endowed funding to remove the uncertainty of operating on outside grant money; the need to include community partnership participation as part of the tenure review for faculty involved in projects such as ESLARP; and the need to replace the model of professional expertise for community development with one of participatory research partnerships. When Reardon left the University of Illinois in 2000 for a faculty position at Cornell University, there was no endowed funding in place for ESLARP. But the success of ESLARP in dealing with the problems of East St. Louis during Reardon's tenure highlighted the work of participating faculty and pointed out the prominence of professional planners (rather than the residents) in urban renewal.

FEMA's job was to manage disasters, but one of Witt's priorities was to manage the disastrous environment of the agency. Witt described an employee walking onto the elevator his first morning on the job: "And this guy comes in, he's carrying a briefcase, and he has his head down looking real gloomy, and I said, hi I'm Jim Lee Witt, and shook my hand and said huh, got on the elevator and went up."[91] The story was a metaphor for an agency hunkered down against an onslaught of criticism without a clear way to make improvements. Communication suffered not only within FEMA, but also with external partners and political overseers. The primary way Witt sought to improve communication was to establish a customer service approach that required every employee to provide the best possible service to every customer. As Witt saw it, the customer service approach not only boosted morale within the agency, but did wonders for creating credible partnerships with FEMA's external partners. To illustrate, Witt related a story. One day when walking around the agency he entered an office where he saw an employee who had just hung up the telephone with a big smile on her face. He asked her why she was so happy, and she related the story of her phone conversation. She had just notified a mayor that the requested flood maps for the mayor's city were in the mail, less than a day after the mayor had asked for them. In the employee's words, the mayor, shocked by the speed of service, said, "Am I really talking to a federal employee?" After telling the story, Witt said, "And the woman telling the story was so happy to have been able to help and to make someone happy. . . . That's what we tried to create."[92]

By treating a wide range of individuals and organizations as customers, Witt sought to build strong partnerships. The key to service and a strong partnership, he believed, was effective and continuous communication. FEMA focused on improving communication with and providing service to victims of disasters, communities, mayors, governors, state emergency management directors, members of Congress, and the numerous organizations involved in disaster relief such as the National Weather Service and U.S. Geological Survey.[93] In his first one hundred days, Witt testified six times before different congressional committees or subcommittees to begin mending bridges burned by FEMA's bumbling performance in handling disasters prior to Witt's tenure. FEMA began working with state and local governments not only to address disasters as they occurred, but also to help prepare for future disasters and to mitigate the losses associated with them. It offered not only information and expertise, but education aimed at preparedness and mitigation as well. And as noted, victims of disaster were given the opportunity to communicate their experiences with FEMA and offer suggestions on how the agency's response could be made better through feedback surveys. Victims of disaster, too, were partners in the effort to build a nationwide approach to preparing for, responding to, and mitigating the consequences of disaster. To build a commitment to open communication, Witt had to build and rebuild communication with external partners and overseers, and he did so by treating each partner like a customer.

To build a community-based approach to policing that would facilitate a program like the CD–CP mental health partnership, Pastore had to turn his energies outward toward the community itself. Community policing would require community cooperation and trust, and both were in short supply when Pastore took office in 1990. As previously noted, Pastore tried to make himself a regular presence in the neighborhoods of New Haven, and he encouraged his officers to do the same. "Policing begins," Pastore noted in an interview, "by getting to know the members of the community on a first-name basis. One of the greatest surprises I had in policing is that the community wants to work with the police."[94]

A large part of building support in the community involved finding ways to mediate different demands placed upon the police that pitted one segment of the community against another. To solve the conflict by making an arrest would only serve to reinforce the skepticism or fear a particular segment of the population might have toward the police. Pastore related a story about a call he received one day from the mayor's office. A group of homeless people had set up a squatter's camp on the New Haven Green—a patch of "sacred ground," as Pastore described it—to protest city budget cuts in programs supporting the homeless population. The city Park Department had received calls from a private committee that maintained the green and wanted the squatters removed. The mayor wanted Pastore to take care of it. Pastore met with the protestors and played cards with them. After a few hands of gin rummy he spoke with them to find out what they wanted and to assure them that he supported their right to protest. They agreed to limit the protest to three more days and to clean up when they were finished, with the guarantee from Pastore that the police would not harass them.[95] By mediating a solution Pastore showed respect for the right of the squatters to protest, but also provided a time limit that the mayor could count upon. It was, in short, outward management efforts that limited the political pressure that could be placed upon the department but also facilitated Pastore's efforts to build rapport and confidence between the police and the community.

These outward efforts by Pastore, Reardon, and Witt targeted and helped to change the environment as a root of program culture. Reardon worked to make a university setting and city government more pliable for the residents, faculty, and students working to build a partnership with shared responsibility as its central commitment. Pastore worked to foster community trust and support for a new policing paradigm that would facilitate a partnership with the Yale Child Study Center devoted to meeting the mental health needs of children exposed to violence. And Witt utilized constant open communication to turn a hostile environment into a supportive one full of potential partners in its pursuit of responding to, mitigating, and preventing disasters across America.

Shared Responsibility

In the effort to manage the roots of culture both within and without a program, managers must understand that the responsibility is one they share with a broad range of participants. An individual leader who is able to assess the existing culture; understand its connections to the environment, task, and resources; and be prepared to work relentlessly for change is essential. But in today's world of public management the authority of a leader is shared among the employees and clientele of the program and other program leaders.[96] A program commitment cannot be changed by dictate from a leader to employees. Employees must embrace and practice the changes sought by a leader. Similarly, a leader cannot dictate changes in an environment of overlapping program jurisdictions, elected officials, and private and nonprofit organizations participating in bringing a policy to fruition. A program commitment changes when all participants involved in a public program embrace the change as an alternative means to do the work.

Kenneth Reardon fostered a change from academic expertise to shared responsibility by practicing participatory research and sharing leadership. Leaders of neighborhood nonprofit organizations and other community-based organizations were very visible and real partners in the leadership effort, but the shared leadership role was extended to every participating resident. An annual camera exercise armed residents with disposable cameras and the instructions to take "nine photographs showing the most valuable and unique qualities of their area; nine photographs revealing the biggest problems confronting their community; and nine photographs highlighting spaces, institutions, and facilities which, if developed, could become important community assets."[97] This camera exercise became the basis of an annual strategic planning process in the neighborhoods and was part of what participants call an empowerment planning process. It was, simply, shared leadership, spreading among all participants the task of identifying problems and strategically planning for the future.

Initiating the CD–CP mental health partnership required shared leadership between Pastore and Donald Cohen and Steven Marans of the Yale University Child Studies Center. Both the Child Studies Center and the Department of Police Services worked to train and inform mental health and police professionals on the needs and circumstances of children exposed to or victimized by violence. Full cooperation from both sides was essential to establish an effective response to the individual mental health needs of a child.

While development and implementation of the CD–CP fellowship programs and seminar training required formal coordination and sharing between leaders of both programs, the actual practice of the partnership on the street required shared leadership with the patrol officers and mental health professionals on the beat. In a review of the initiative, both police officers and mental health professionals reported real changes in police practice involving children and violence, both at the scene and in clinical practice. "When they are not the only professionals contending with the aftermath of violence and when they attend to the emotional needs of children and families and deliver direct services, officers feel they have a new way of 'taking control' of highly disturbing situations."[98] Police officers thus were empowered to focus on managing a stressful situation, and to work on building trust and respect with members of the community. Similarly, mental health professionals reported a deeper understanding of the situations surrounding community violence, and came to rely upon the police as a valuable community resource. When the partnerships were put into practice at the scene of violence, police officers were empowered to work more openly and effectively with community members, and mental health professionals had better and more insightful information about the families involved. The partnership created leadership opportunities among officers and clinicians on the street seeking to craft clinical responses for the mental health needs of individual children.

Finally, James Lee Witt shared the re-creation of FEMA's culture with agency employees. When Witt brought senior management together at the retreat, he empowered them to think about mission definition, organizational design, and goals and priorities for the agency. "I didn't stay with them. I went back on the last day to hear what they had come up with. You would have been amazed. They all came together and worked hard on it. They made a one year list of what we were going to accomplish—and we accomplished everything on that list."[99] Witt's delegation of authority created another opportunity to enhance communication within FEMA by enhancing trust. By extending the authority for identifying goals to top managers, he demonstrated his trust in them. His actions also placed responsibility for better communication and ultimately better performance with his senior managers. In these ways he shared the role of leader in rebuilding FEMA culture and performance.

BEING RELENTLESS

Changes in culture must be pursued relentlessly. To make ESLARP a success, Kenneth Reardon had to continuously practice the changes that he wanted to bring about and routinely review critically his and his colleague's efforts to ensure that their approach was sound and their results solid. Participatory research necessitates a complete shift away from the system of meaning that defines the work of many university-based academics. Community residents become partners in the research effort rather than the subjects of research. Responsibility for defining the problems, researching and analyzing solutions, and implementing those solutions is shared equally between residents and academics. And the knowledge drawn from the experience of actually living life in a particular community is as valuable to developing solutions to community problems as the expertise of academic training.

In order to make these changes a reality, Reardon had to share power daily. Perhaps most importantly, he had to insure that all participants would have the opportunity to evaluate, comment, and help to change the direction of ESLARP. When residents accused Reardon and his colleagues in 1995 of being "racist, sexist, and colonialist" in their approach to training ESLARP participants, Reardon and the others were initially hurt and shocked. Wasn't the program a success? Wasn't there an equal partnership in the research, planning, and implementation effort? No, according to the residents. A real partnership would provide equal learning and training opportunities. Residents participating in ESLARP programs needed equal access to university classes. Reardon's response? The residents were right, and the Neighborhood College was established.

Nearly every year that Reardon led the project, residents, faculty, and students gathered for a retreat to evaluate the program through structured reflection. In 1998 the retreat was extended an extra day. Sixty leaders from East St. Louis were present, and the central issue was, "Should we declare victory and go home, should we continue with the same effort, but a little differently, or should we more deeply embrace [a different approach]?"[100] Participants were just about to pat each other on the back for a job well done when an older teacher from the community stood up and said, "With a growing increase in youth poverty, how can we say we are done?" "It was a bomb," said Reardon.[101] The commitment to the program continued, with renewed efforts to address child poverty.

Reardon and other participating faculty sought opportunities to expand the influence and power of residents in other venues as well. In 1998 several community women developed a method to evaluate community redevelopment efforts in East St. Louis. They presented their method in a forum called the Resident Panel at the annual COPC meeting held in East St. Louis that summer. The evaluation technique was unprecedented, according to Reardon, in that it included the community and its direct evaluation of the efforts. With respect to the ESLARP efforts, the evaluators identified the participatory method as a strength of the program, but encouraged the university to reach deeper into the community to broaden participation, and to focus on training the youth in the community as future leaders. With respect to HUD, sponsor of COPC, the evaluators recommended sponsoring a "residents only" conference to allow residents to compare ideas and experiences, and to provide travel money for residents to visit other COPC sites for peer interaction and learning.[102]

In addition to practicing equal access to decision making, training, and participation, Reardon practiced the language of participatory research. Rarely did Reardon use the word "I" when discussing ESLARP. The efforts were mutual, involving "we" and "us." He spoke of his own education, what he had learned from the residents individually and collectively. He spoke of the privilege and honor to know and work with people like Ceola Davis, one of the first community leaders willing to participate with Reardon in the effort. And he spoke of the responsibility of universities to "bring faculty out of the ivory towers . . . [bring] benefits to the community . . . [and rediscover] the soul and the special role of the university in the commons."[103]

James Lee Witt's tenure with FEMA represented a relentless, eight-year effort to open the lines of communication within FEMA as well as those without. From his first days on the job, Witt worked to improve the opportunities and ways in which FEMA employees could communicate with each other and with him. His efforts to improve communication with external partners and political overseers was similarly constant throughout his tenure. To maintain open communication as a central commitment of FEMA culture required daily management of the way FEMA's environmental partners interacted with the agency, the way the agency communicated its role to FEMA employees and to its partners, and the way FEMA deployed and used its resources within these partnerships. Witt maintained contact with members of Congress responsible for FEMA's authorization and appropriations, as well as with members whose states and districts were affected by disasters or were likely to be affected. In two days in the summer of 1993 Witt called every member of Congress in nine midwestern states affected by flooding. "You have to reach out . . . I told them what we were doing, and that if they had a problem, to call me."[104] And they did. From time to time members of Congress contacted Witt for assistance on a program in their district or state. Even if FEMA had no legislative authority to participate in the program, Witt would gather information and contact people in other programs who could help and then arrange a meeting to bring the parties together.[105]

From the hosting of "hurricane summits" and the coordination of state and federal efforts in the event of a hurricane to the open and respectful offer of FEMA assistance to states, Witt constantly sought to improve communication as a means to improve FEMA's performance. Good communication, Witt understood, required not only that FEMA speak to its partners, but that it listen to them as well. Some states are better prepared than others to deal with disasters. Witt worked to make his agency and its resources available to all states, as they needed and requested it. The point was to know the different state disaster relief systems and personnel, and to build partnerships before disasters hit. Finally, Witt used communication with the American public to try to shift some of the responsibility for dealing with natural disasters to the public itself. He believed that FEMA had a role in educating people about where to build homes and businesses—not on flood planes or in the path of predictable hurricanes—and encouraging people to take responsibility for their building decisions. This shift of responsibility is clearly articulated in his comments before the press club in 1998:

> We are considering denying national flood insurance to homeowners who have filed two or more claims that total more than the value of their home and refuse to elevate their home, refuse to flood-proof their home, or refuse to accept

a buy-out relocation offer. People need to accept the responsibility and the consequences of their choice to live in high-risk areas. We should charge people who live in high-risk areas the fair market rates for insurance, instead of the lower, subsidized federal flood insurance rates.[106]

Witt's strategy for building open communication is simply stated: "You have to try to be open, honest, straightforward, and listen. We have to learn to do more listening."[107] And he was continuously available to listen. Witt woke up at 4:30 a.m. to arrive at the office by 6:30, and over an eight-year period he didn't finish a single vacation. But his continuous attention to the ways in which his agency's environment, task, and resources wove together paid off: Witt was able to establish at FEMA a culture committed to open communication and customer service.

Nicholas Pastore was similarly relentless in his efforts to create a department committed to understanding and respecting the community and to developing and maintaining professional partnerships. At one point early in his tenure Pastore had more requests from private and nonprofit organizations and groups to create police partnerships than the department had the capacity to undertake. "We didn't have the experience to deal with all the help," Pastore recalled. "Officers could eat Dunkin' Donuts and when the bell goes off, respond. . . . We weren't ready."[108] But Pastore was relentless in trying to build that capacity—to make his department ready. He continuously articulated and practiced an alternative approach to policing, one that required the officers to understand and connect with all members of the community in order to serve them. He "vented," and then continuously pursued alternative training methods that could foster an understanding of the community and how partnerships could grow. And as the capacity for community-based policing grew, he worked to support the types of partnerships, such as the CD–CP mental health program, that he viewed as key to sustaining a community-based approach to policing. The CD–CP mental health partnership was based upon the premise that when police play an active and informed role in the treatment of children exposed to violence, they play a role in mitigating and even preventing future violence as well as facilitating the healing of a child undergoing treatment. Pastore understood this and was relentless in trying to find ways to empower patrol officers to play a role in resolving or dealing with problems in a neighborhood beat, drawing particularly upon training techniques and exposure and contact with special populations.

CAPITALIZING ON AND INSTITUTIONALIZING CHANGE

Finally, managers working to change the integration of the roots of culture must find ways to institutionalize the changes, or make them a more routine part of program practice. The changes sought by Pastore were institutionalized through a training regime clearly illustrated in the CD–CP mental health partnership that was built around five basic program components: a ten-week seminar for new police recruits, child development fellowships for police supervisors, police fellowships for clinicians, a weekly case conference between mental health professionals and police officers, and a twenty-four-hour beeper service giving police officers immediate access to mental health clinicians. The commitment on the part of the Department of Police Services to include the training for new recruits and to require participation in the fellowships for supervisors injected the community-based mental health perspective into the professional development and identification of officers. New police officers engaging with children and families for the first time on a daily basis learned to think about children's development and the way they might influence children. Similarly, supervisors were expected to be able to translate the concepts of community policing and the mental health partnership into practice.[109] Finally, the weekly case conference was an opportunity to reinforce the partnership on a face-to-face level, and to problem solve in a collaborative forum. Participation in each piece of the program deepened the commitments to understanding the community and professional partnerships as a means to establish a community approach to children's mental health needs.

Within ESLARP, the faculty executive committee, university studios and classes, the Neighborhood College, NTAC, and the community organizer worked to institutionalize the commitment to participatory research, direct action organizing, and popular education. The Emerson Park Community Development Corporation, the Winstanley/Industry Neighborhood Community Development Corporation, and numerous community-based organizations that together formed ESLCAN worked to institutionalize the planning, organizing, and implementation capacity of community organizations in East St. Louis. But ultimately the stability of shared responsibility as a central commitment of ESLARP will rest with the willingness of future ESLARP leaders to relentlessly practice shared power leadership and push the university and political environments toward acceptance of the participatory research approach.

Similarly, the stability of Witt's push to institutionalize open communication and customer service throughout FEMA rests in part with the continued efforts of FEMA leaders to honor those program commitments. Witt made communication with his employees, the public, and FEMA's partners a routine dimension of the agency's operations. Weekly newsletters and weekly opportunities to meet with the director, public feedback surveys, and the creation of numerous forums to meet with and discuss disaster issues with FEMA's partners all facilitated and fostered open communication as a central component of FEMA's culture. Similarly, reward systems that honored innovation in customer service and a new training program helped to institutionalize the commitment to serving all of FEMA's customers in a continuously improving manner. But routinization must be accompanied by the willingness of future FEMA leaders to practice the commitment to open communication and customer service.

CONCLUSION

The cases in this chapter depict public managers changing cultures by changing the way task, resources, and environments fold together within public programs. The leaders of ESLARP, FEMA, and the CD–CP mental health partnership, alone and in concert with others, accomplished these changes by practicing six strategies.

First, they identified the existing commitments of the culture and, second, the connections between those commitments and the roots of culture. Reardon identified academic expertise as the core commitment of UEMAP, deeply embedded in a complex environment of university practices and city politics, professional skills and practices, and limited monetary resources to tackle the onerous task of finding ways to stabilize and revitalize the city of East St. Louis. At FEMA, James Lee Witt saw commitments to minimal communication and to the work of individual programs linked to the lack of clarity about what the agency was to accomplish and how, and a hostile political environment that grew more hostile with each botched effort to provide disaster relief. And Chief of Police Pastore and physicians at Yale University identified the commitments to professional responsibility after the fact and clinic-based treatment as roadblocks to effecting a more productive way of addressing the needs of kids exposed to violence. Both commitments were embedded in professional practices built around long-term understandings of the task at hand—policing and mental health counseling. The commitment to policing as a response to crime, in particular, was embedded in an increasingly violent environment that fostered a military response from police and nurtured militaristic police training techniques.

Third, leaders of ESLARP, FEMA, and the CD–CP mental health partnership thought about what needed to change, and then articulated the change. James Lee Witt spoke about, and continuously practiced, open communication within the agency, with FEMA's outside partners, and with the agency's political overseers. He emphasized the importance of understanding and serving FEMA's customers—from victims of disaster to state emergency management agencies and nonprofit organizations involved in disaster relief. Nick Pastore and other leaders in the CD–CP mental health partnership emphasized the importance of working beyond professional boundaries to better serve children exposed to violence. The New Haven police force and mental health professionals at Yale University created a forum for the articulation of the commitments to understanding and working with the community and forging professional partnerships to better serve the needs of children in the community. And Ken Reardon's persistence in discussing and writing about the value of participatory research as a means to building a commitment to shared responsibility and the importance of continuous evaluation of the work of ESLARP provided a vision for how the program could tackle the problems of East St. Louis neighborhoods.

Fourth, each leader approached the management of cultural roots as an inward, outward, and shared responsibility and, fifth, each leader was relentless in his effort to demonstrate and practice the changes he sought. Reardon, Witt, and Pastore worked not only to change the way participants understood the program task and applied resources and skills but also to address the program environment. In partnership with the residents of East St. Louis, colleagues, and students, Reardon relentlessly engaged university administrators and city officials to eliminate barriers to participatory research and the commitment to shared responsibility. In partnership with FEMA employees and emergency personnel and support groups around the country, Witt relentlessly built bridges, articulated a clear task for FEMA, and promoted a focus on the customer. And Pastore, in partnership with other police leaders and faculty from Yale University, worked to bridge two distinct professions and program environments to build a new program. In order to integrate task, resources, and a very complex environment in a manner that would support community-based mental health treatment, they had to relentlessly manage the training, experiences, and ultimately the environment within which police officers and mental health professionals conducted their work.

Finally, the leaders of ESLARP, FEMA, and the CD–CP mental health partnership sought opportunities to institutionalize changes in the roots of culture wherever possible. ESLARP established a technical support office staffed with a direct action organizer in the city of East St. Louis to facilitate the work of residents and organizations as partners with shared responsibility. FEMA established customer training for all employees, and published an agency-wide newspaper and "rumor mill" to build on the commitment to open communication. And exposure to mental health issues and the lives and concerns of people in New Haven neighborhoods became a routine part of police training. Each leader found a variety of ways to entrench or institutionalize the effort to reintegrate the roots of program culture.

Each of the changes in program commitments eventually provided participants with a guide for action, or rules for getting the job done. A commitment to shared responsibility in ESLARP provided each faculty, student, and resident with a clear indication of how every decision should be made, every action taken, and every step executed to train and prepare for the project. A commitment to open communication in FEMA provided employees and FEMA partners with a means to tackle responses to disaster, as well as to begin changing the way the nation prepares for and mitigates disasters. Through open communication with employees and a focus on its customers, FEMA came to an understanding of how best to reorganize the agency and to better perform its responsibilities. And the commitment to understanding the community and to professional partnerships gave police officers in New Haven an alternative way to see their role in preventing and dealing with violence and area mental health clinicians a new view of their role in treating victims of violence.

Each change in program commitments provided glue to the work of public programs spread across organizations, government and private sectors, and cities and the country. The ESLARP focus on shared responsibility created a center point for university and East St. Louis participants. Shared responsibility became a point of identity for participants—some located in Urbana–Champaign, others in East St. Louis. Open communication connected FEMA internally and with its partners in every state of the country. Witt's constant emphasis on communication to assess what FEMA was doing, and to find out what it could do better, created links that did not previously exist between partners. And the commitments to understanding the community and to professional partnerships linked two previously unconnected programs—policing and mental health—and created bridges with other community service providers as both groups of professionals began to see the ways in which a community-based approach could offer a range of alternatives for kids exposed to violence.

Notes

1. The case is made for a change in ESLARP culture in the body of this chapter. For discussions of the progressive changes made in ESLARP throughout the 1990s and the basic challenges faced by the program, see Kenneth Reardon, "Institutionalizing Community Service Learning at a Major Research University: The Case of the East St. Louis Action Research Project," *Michigan Journal of Community Service Learning* 4 (1997): 130–136.

2. The argument that FEMA's culture was changed is made in the body of this chapter. Jerry Ellig makes the case for a culture change in FEMA as well. See Ellig, *Results-Based management at the Federal Emergency Management Agency: A Case Study in the Public Sector Leadership Project,* Mercatus Center, George Mason University (March 29, 2000), 25–29. For an overview of Witt's leadership and the improved performance of the agency see GovernmentExec.com, "Mastering Disaster" (February 1999). Retrieved from the Web on April 18, 2001, at http://www.govexec.com/gpp/0299fema.htm.

3. The CD–CP mental health partnership is the third case illustrated in this chapter. For an in-depth discussion of the ideas and effort behind the program and the changes the program has prompted in the Department of Police Services and in mental health clinical practices, see Steven Marans, in collaboration with Jean Adnopoz, Miriam Berkman, Dean Esserman, Douglas MacDonald, Steven Nagler, Richard Randall, Mark Schaefer, and Melvin Wearing, *The Police–Mental Health Partnership: A Community-Based Response to Urban Violence* (New Haven: Yale University Press, 1995).

4. Barbara Romzek and Melvin Dubnick, "Accountability in the Public Sector: Lessons from the Challenger Tragedy," *Public Administration Review* 47 (1987): 227–238.

5. For an excellent portrayal of the difficulties of managing a public program of great interest to elected officials, see Martha Derthick, *Agency Under Stress: The Social Security Administration in American Government* (Washington, D.C.: Brookings, 1990). Derthick's analysis of the Social Security Administration's efforts to implement the Supplemental Security Income program and the review of disability insurance cases demonstrates the collision of organizational capacity and management concerns with the ambitions and motivations of members of Congress and the president.

6. Richard Fenno, *Home Style: House Members in Their Districts* (Glenview, Ill.: Scott, Foresman, 1978), 249.

7. The term is Robert Behn's in "Management by Groping Along," *Journal of Policy Analysis and Management* 7, no. 4 (1988): 643–663.

8. Ibid.

9. Anne Khademian, *Checking on Banks: Autonomy and Accountability in Three Federal Agencies* (Washington, D.C.: Brookings, 1996), 116–127.

10. General Accounting Office, *Civil Defense: FEMA's Management Controls Need Strengthening,* Report to the Chairman, Subcommittee on Military Installations and Facilities, Committee on Armed Servies, House of Representatives, GAO/NSIAD-88–52, December 1987, 8–9.

11. National Academy of Public Administration, *Coping with Catastrophe: Building an Emergency Management System to Meet People's Needs in Natural and Manmade Disasters* (Washington, D.C.: NAPA, February 1993), 42–43. For a similar assessment of FEMA's condition, see Sandra Schneider, *Flirting with Disaster: Public Management in Crisis Situations* (Armonk, N.Y.: M. E. Sharpe, 1995).

12. James Lee Witt, "Closing Plenary. Leadership: Communicating Our Leadership to the Public," National Park Service General Conference, Discovery 2000, September 11–15, 2000. Retrieved from the Web January 2001 at www.nps.gov/discovery2000/leader/plenary-2.htm.

13. James Lee Witt, telephone interview with the author, October 24, 2001.

14. Witt, "Closing Plenary."

15. Ibid.

16. Ellig, *Results-Based Management,* 29–32.

17. Kenneth Reardon, "Enhancing the Capacity of Community-Based Organizations in East St. Louis," *Journal of Planning Education and Research* 17 (1998): 323–333; and Reardon, "Participatory Action Research and Real Community-Based Planning in East St. Louis, Illinois," in *Building Community: Social Science in Action,* ed. P. Nyden, A. Figert, M. Shibley, and D. Burrows (Thousand Oaks, Calif.: Pine Forge Press, 1997), 233.

18. Witt, interview.

19. Alasdair Roberts, *The Master of Disaster: James Lee Witt and the Federal Emergency Management Agency* (Washington, D.C.: Council for Excellence in Government, April 1997).

20. Nicholas Pastore, telephone interview with the author, November 12, 2001.

21. Marans, *The Police–Mental Health Partnership,* 8.

22. New Haven Department of Police Services web page, "Child Development–Community Policing Program." Retrieved from the web on April 20, 2001 at http://www.newhavenpolice.org/.

23. Erwin Hargrove and John Glidewell, eds., *Impossible Jobs in Public Management* (Lawrence: University Press of Kansas, 1990).

24. Ibid., 45.

25. Kenneth Reardon, "Creating a Community/University Partnership That Works: The Case of the East St. Louis Action Research Project," *Metropolitan Universities: An International Forum* 6, no. 2 (1995): 49.

26. Reardon, "Enhancing the Capacity of Community Based Organizations," 324.

27. Reardon, "Creating a Community/University Partnership That Works," 55.

28. Ibid., 54–55.

29. Ibid., 53.

30. Reardon, "Enhancing the Capacity of Community Based Organizations," 331.

31. Reardon, "Institutionalizing Community Service Learning," 135.

32. Kenneth Reardon, telephone interview with the author, November 3, 2000.

33. Reardon, "Institutionalizing Community Service Learning."

34. Reardon, "Creating a Community/University Partnership," 55.

35. Reardon, interview.

36. United States Department of Housing and Urban Development web site, "Community Outreach Partnership Centers Program," Program Description. Retrieved from the Web on April 20, 2001, at http://www.hud.gov/local/sea/sean2k32.html.

37. Office of University Partnerships, Grant Recipients. Retrieved from the web on April 20, 2001, at http://www.oup.org/about/grantccscopc.html.

38. Reardon, interview. Reardon argues that residents of the communities impacted by COPC grants are yet to be included as regular participants in the national COPC conferences. The announcement for the 2001 National Conference identified potential participants as "COPC grantees, academic leaders (presidents, deans and department chairs), community partners, and other interested parties." Retrieved from the web on April 20, 2001, at http://www.oup.org/confer/confer.html. When the meeting was held in East St. Louis in 1998, residents of the city presented a panel based upon a model to evaluate community redevelopment efforts. See below.

39. John Ellig reports that between 1982 and 1992 FEMA spent twelve times as much money preparing for a nuclear disaster than preparing for natural disasters. See Ellig, *Results-Based Management,* 8. See also General Accounting Office, *Civil Defense: FEMA's Management Controls,* 8–9; and General Accounting Office, *The Federal Role in Hurricane Preparedness Planning,* Statement of J. Dexter Peach, Director Resources, Community and Economic Development Division before the Subcommittee on Legislation and National Security of the Committee on Government Operations, House of Representatives, GAO/RCED-83-182, May 5, 1983, 10–13.

40. For a discussion of the management challenges facing FEMA, see General Accounting Office, "Statement of Lowell Dodge, Associate Director, Resources, Community and Economic Development Division, Before the Subcommittee on Science, Research and Technology of the Committee on Science and Technology, House of Representatives, on FEMA's Implementation of the Earthquake Hazards Reduction Act of 1977," As Amended (March 3, 1983, before the Senate, 120702, and March 15, 1983, 120802).

41. Quoted in Robert Worth, "Reinvention Lite—Why Al Gore Still Has a Long Way to Go," *Washington Monthly,* September 1998. Posted on October 4, 2000, by L.N. Smithee, at http://www.freerepublic.com/forum/a39db1c1e2a04.htm.

42. Quoted in Roberts, *Master of Disaster,* 1.

43. See "A Lesson in Violence," transcript from News Hour, October 15, 1998. Retrieved from the Web January 2001 at http://www.pbs.org/newshour/bb/education/july-dec98/violence_10-15.html.

44. Terry Moe argues that interest groups competing to define the way a government agency is structured and operated might go so far as to identify with professional groups that approach a public policy issue in a manner favorable to the interest group. See Moe, "The Politics of Bureaucratic Structure," in *Can the Government Govern?* ed. J. Chubb and P. Peterson (Washington, D.C.: Brookings, 1989).

45. Frederick Mosher, *Democracy and the Public Service* (Oxford: Oxford University Press, 1982).

46. See, for example, Harold Laswell, "The Policy Orientation," in *The Policy Sciences,* ed. D. Lerner and H. Laswell (Palo Alto: Stanford University Press, 1951), 3–15.

47. Marans, *The Police–Mental Health Partnership,* 8.

48. "A Lesson in Violence."

49. Ellig, *Results-Based Management,* 8.

50. General Accounting Office, *Civil Defense,* 8.

51. General Accounting Office, "Statement of John Luke, Associate Director of Resources, Community, and Economic Development Division, before the Subcommittee on Investigations and Oversight of the Committee on Science and Technology House of Representatives, on Recent Management Practices at the Federal Emergency Management Agency," August 1, 1984, 124792; and General Accounting Office, "Statement of Lowell Dodge before the Subcommittee on Science, Technology and Space of the Committee on Commerce, Science and Transportation, Senate," March 3, 1983, 12072.

52. Witt, "Closing Plenary."

53. Pastore, interview.

54. These past programs included the War on Poverty, Model Cities, Planned Variations, and the Community Development Block Grant programs.

55. Reardon, "Creating a Community/University Partnership," 49.

56. Reardon, "Enhancing the Capacity of Community-Based Organizations," 325. For an in-depth discussion of participatory research, see Kenneth Reardon and Thomas Shields, "Promoting Sustainable Community/University Partnerships Through Participatory Action Research," *National Society for Experiential Education Quarterly* 23, no. 1 (1997): 1, 22–25.

57. The concept of direct action organizing is articulated in Saul Alinsky, *Rules for Radicals: A Practical Primer for Realistic Radicals* (New York: Vintage Press, 1971).

58. Kenneth Reardon, "An Experiential Approach to Creating a Community/University Partnership That Works: The East St. Louis Action Research Project," unpublished manuscript, 8.

59. Witt, interview.

60. Witt, "Closing Plenary."

61. Ibid.

62. Cited in Ellig, *Results-Based Management,* 8.

63. National Partnership for Reinventing Government, "In Recovery: Federal Emergency Management Agency." Retrieved from the Web on November 27, 2001, at http://govinfo.library.unt.edu/npr/library/status/sec2c.htm.

64. "Mastering Disaster," 3, cited in Ellig, *Results-Based Management,* 25.

65. Witt, "Closing Plenary."

66. Pastore, interview.

67. "Pastore: The Transition from Hustler to Top Cop," *Yale Daily News,* March 20, 1995. Retrieved from the web on November 26, 2001, at http://www.yale.edu/ydn/paper/3.20/3.20.95storyno.QB.html.

68. "About Nicholas Pastore, CJPF Research Fellow in Police Policy." Retrieved from the Web in November 2000 at http://www.cjpf.org/newhaven/.

69. Pastore, interview.

70. Ibid.

71. Ibid.

72. Ibid.

73. Ibid.

74. Drug Policy Foundation, interview with Nick Pastore, *Drug Policy Letter* (spring 1998). Retrieved from the Web November 2000 at http://www.cjpf.org/newhaven/pastore.html.

75. Ibid.

76. Marans, *The Police–Mental Health Partnership.*

77. Quote posted on the East St. Louis Action Research Project web site, "Farmers Market." Retrieved from the Web on April 22, 2001, at http://www.ESLARP.uiuc.edu/overview/doc5.htm.

78. Reardon, interview.

79. Quoted in Reardon, "Enhancing the Capacity of Community-Based Organizations," 326.

80. Neighborhood Technical Assistance Center, *Annual Report,* August 5, 1996–August 5, 1997, submitted by Damon Y. Smith, Project Coordinator. See section 1.

81. Quote posted on the East St. Louis Action Research Project web site, "Farmers Market."

82. Reardon, interview.

83. Quoted in Roberts, *Master of Disaster.*

84. Ellig, *Results-Based Management,* 10, 18–22.

85. Witt, "Closing Plenary."

86. Ellig, *Results-Based Management,* 18.

87. Witt, "Closing Plenary."

88. Witt, interview; see also Ellig, *Results-Based Management,* 21–22.

89. Reardon, "Enhancing the Capacity of Community-Based Organizations," 326.

90. Reardon, interview.

91. Witt, "Closing Plenary."

92. Witt, interview.

93. See, for example, "Remarks of James Lee Witt, Federal Emergency Management Agency, Before the Midyear Meeting of the National Emergency

Management Association, Crystal City, Va., February 26, 1996." Retrieved from the Web January 2001 at http://www.fema.gov/library/wittspch12.htm. See also Ellig, *Results-Based Management*, 29–33.

94. Drug Policy Foundation, interview with Nick Pastore.

95. Pastore, interview.

96. John Bryson and Barbara Crosby, *Leadership for the Common Good: Tackling Public Problems in a Shared Power World* (San Francisco: Jossey-Bass, 1995).

97. Kenneth Reardon and Thomas Shields, "Promoting Sustainable Community/University Partnerships Through Participatory Action Research," *National Society for Experiential Education Quarterly* 23, no. 1 (1997): 24.

98. Marans, *The Police–Mental Health Partnership*, 108.

99. Witt, "Closing Plenary."

100. Reardon, interview.

101. Ibid.

102. East St. Louis Action Research Project, "Town and Gown: A Resident Evaluation of a Community Outreach Partnership Center." Resident Panel Presentation at the Community Outreach Partnership Center Conference, East St. Louis, Illinois, September 24–25, 1998. Retrieved from the Web on April 23, 2001 at http://www.eslarp.uiuc.edu/copc/panel.htm.

103. Reardon, interview.

104. Quoted in Roberts, *Master of Disaster.*

105. Witt, interview.

106. Transcript of National Press Club Luncheon featuring James L. Witt, Director, Federal Emergency Management Agency, November 10, 1998. Retrieved from the Web January 2001at http://www.fema.gov/library/wittspch9.htm.

107. Witt, interview.

108. Pastore, interview.

109. Marans, *The Police–Mental Health Partnership*, 40–61.

4

Extending the Cultural
Roots Model

IN CHAPTER 2 WE EXAMINED the debate between advocates of managed culture change and their critics, the skeptics. The advocates, who draw their arguments largely from the world of business, contend that the culture of an organization can be changed through the efforts of a manager. The skeptics, who challenge this assertion, draw largely from the realm of public policy management. In Chapter 3, we developed the cultural roots model, a framework for effecting change in organizations that links the roots of culture—task, resources, and environment—to culture change. In this chapter we will delve deeper into our framework to assess the capacity of the cultural roots model to predict culture change in organizations. In so doing, we must answer the following four key questions:

1. Can commitments, even a single commitment, capture the essence of culture?
2. Is the environment always a factor in culture?
3. Can the roots of any culture be managed?
4. Do culture changes stick when leaders leave?

To answer these questions, we will look at the experiences of U.S. bank regulatory agencies, the South African Police Service, the Securities and Exchange Commission, and the administration of higher education in the United States.

CAPTURING THE ESSENCE OF CULTURE

Among anthropologists, sociologists, political scientists, and economists there is broad disagreement over how to conceptualize culture—how to discuss what it is and the role that culture might play in a group, organization, or society.[1] Even when researchers can agree on the role culture can or might play in an organization or program, there is still disagreement over what to look for, or how to identify culture. Perhaps the most widely known model of culture is Edgar Schein's three-level analysis.[2] As discussed in Chapter 2, Schein divides culture into three levels.[2] Level 1 consists of "artifacts," or the most visible dimensions of a culture. Organization or program symbols, ceremonies, celebrations, art, patterns of communication, stories, and technology all give a glimpse into culture. Level 2 consists of "values and beliefs," or what members believe "ought to be" in the work of their organization or program. Ideologies, attitudes, and philosophies are the manifestation of culture at Level 2. Finally, at Level 3, the deepest and most unconscious level of culture, are "basic assumptions" that capture fundamental notions of how the organization or program and participants relate to the environment, time, space, reality, and each other.

In a remarkably comprehensive study of organizational culture, J. Steven Ott examines the numerous ways in which research projects identify the concept of culture and then categorizes them within the Schein framework of three levels. The result is a matrix with the levels of culture across the top, various manifestations of culture along the side, and in the body of the matrix an indication of where a particular manifestation of culture falls within the levels of culture (see Table 4.1). A study that examined feelings or ideology as a source of culture, for example, would be focusing on Level 2 components of culture, while a study that examined symbols, stories, or language would be focusing on Level 1 components of culture. Here, Schein's framework provides managers with a means for dissecting the dimensions of culture by focusing on each level, and looking for elements that fit within each level. "[T]he matrix can assist a manager or a student to begin matching alternative methods for changing or reinforcing an organizational culture with his or her purpose for doing so."[3]

As a tool for thinking about culture in the abstract, this framework can be very useful. It is perhaps not as useful, however, for the public manager with little time to conduct research differentiating between the three levels of culture within a program or organization. Even for the researcher who can devote her or his full attention to the analysis of a culture, differentiating between a "basic assumption," for example, and a "value" or a "belief" is quite difficult, and perhaps unnecessary for a basic understanding of culture and how its roots might be managed. How does one distinguish between a belief system that is out of consciousness—a Level 3 basic assumption—and one that is consciously held—a Level 2 dimension of culture? A young participant in ESLARP might hold a belief system about race, class, and urban poverty that is out of consciousness, embedded deeply enough within him or her to form a basic assumption guiding his or her participation in the program. An older, more seasoned participant in the program, however, might consciously hold the very same belief system, using it purposefully to focus and guide his or her work with ESLARP. Experience in the program, educational opportunities, participation in national conferences, and numerous other activities might have served to bring the basic assumption to a more focused, conscious level where it guides the participant's understanding of the work ESLARP ought to do and how it should do it. How should we make the

Table 4.1 Matching Schein's Levels of Culture with Different Elements of Culture

Elements of Organizational culture	Artifacts (Level 1)	Beliefs and values (Level 2)	Basic assumptions (Level 3)
Art	*		
Attitudes		*	
Celebration	*		
Commitment to excellence		*	
Communication patterns	*		
Ethics		*	
Feelings		*	
Glue that holds an organization together			*
Heroes	*		
Historical vestiges	*		
Ideologies		*	
Justification for behavior		*	
Language	*		
Meanings		*	
Mindset		*	*
Philosophy		*	*
Physical arrangements	*		
Purpose		*	
Spirit			*
Stories	*		
Symbols	*		
Tacit understandings		*	
Tradition	*		
Vision		*	
Worldviews		*	*

Source: Adapted from J. Steven Ott, *The Organizational Culture Perspective* (Pacific Grove, Calif.: Brooks/Cole; 1989), Figure 3-4. Ott's matrix includes more categories of cultural elements, as well as a variation on the levels of culture. Specifically, he includes a level between "artifacts" and "beliefs and values" that he calls "patterns of behavior."

classification? Similarly, how are we to distinguish a symbol or an artifact from a value or belief that motivates behavior? A solvent bank insurance fund is not only a powerful symbol of the work of the Federal Deposit Insurance Corporation (Level 1), but a motivating factor as well (Level 2)—a solvent fund is essential to the integrity and capacity of the agency.

All of this is not to say that classification along Schein's levels is not possible or desirable. It is to say, however, that there must be an easier way. Perhaps the reduction of culture to "commitments" slights the nuanced differences between artifacts, values, and basic assumptions that are critical for capturing the complexities of culture. Skeptics might argue that numerous, sometimes contradictory, commitments can define a culture, or even distinct cultures within the same program. What one manager or observer identifies as a commitment might miss the depth of conflict or variety of differences that exists within a program. And perhaps the condensation of culture to commitments rolls over conceptual elements of culture that are crucial to advance attitudes toward program and organizational culture with the broader study of culture in societies. But for purposes of understanding culture as a means to enhance the performance of public programs, our focus on commitments seems appropriate.

In each of the programs discussed in Chapter 3, public managers sought to change the way work was done. They did so by articulating and continuously communicating an idea or concept that guided efforts to manage the integration of task, resources, and complex environments. Through their efforts to manage this process of integration, they relentlessly practiced a commitment to shared responsibility and continuous evaluation (in the case of ESLARP), open communication and dedication to the customer (in the case of FEMA), and understanding the community and professional partnerships (in the case of the CD–CP mental health partnership).

Regardless of how deeply these commitments are held by participants, how many participants embrace possible alternative understandings of the work they do, or whether the concepts are consciously or unconsciously held, these key commitments matter for the way work is done in ESLARP, FEMA, and the CD–CP mental health partnership. One evaluation of the CD–CP mental health partnership concludes that a new understanding of professional policing has taken hold in the New Haven Department of Police Service. Through their training and work experience with mental health clinicians, officers report an ability to "take control" of situations acting as "benign figures of authority who help to reestablish a semblance of stability in the midst of the emotional chaos."[4] And as officers have built supportive relationships with children and families, they have been able to build trust with families and neighborhoods that facilitate crime prevention.[5] Similarly, the commitment to understanding the community and professional partnerships has changed the way mental health professionals understand and conceive of treatment options for kids and their understanding of the role police can play in treatment.[6] FEMA's performance turnaround, its efforts to educate the public in prevention and mitigation, its establishment of broad and strong partnerships across the country to facilitate disaster relief, and its remarkable reputation in Congress all are illustrations of FEMA's commitments to customer service and open communication. And the constantly evolving nature of ESLARP under Kenneth Reardon's leadership toward an engaged partnership is testimony to the strength of shared responsibility and continuous evaluation as program commitments. Residents constantly challenged and succeeded in improving the "shared" nature of the work and the rewards, both within the ESLARP program and in the greater planning community.

In short, whether or not "commitments" capture the essence of what others identify as culture, they are the informal guides to the way work is done in a program.

THE ENVIRONMENT AS A FACTOR: BANK REGULATORY AGENCIES IN THE UNITED STATES

Advocates for managing culture usually identify the environment as an important variable to be monitored so leaders can make changes in culture to adjust to changes in environment. The framework presented in this book goes further by suggesting that the environment is directly connected to culture and must be part of any management effort to change culture, particularly in the political world of public organizations. But there are agencies in the public sector operating with relative autonomy, generally free of the scrutiny and oversight of political superiors. Such organizations would seem to minimize if not eliminate altogether the argument for including the environment as an explicit variable or root of culture. On the contrary, the environment is always a factor. It is precisely the careful management of the environment that allows agencies to maintain cultures that in turn sustain autonomy.

A key responsibility of a leader is to maintain the organization by both protecting and enhancing agency autonomy.[7] Agencies with particularly popular and precise missions, with clear and simple indicators of good performance and singular expertise to conduct complex tasks, will have high levels of political autonomy. Organizations with vague mandates, divided constituencies, "hired" expertise, and no clear indicators of performance will suffer the onslaught of political oversight and investigation.[8] Leaders can also work to enhance autonomy by seeking out tasks not being conducted by other organizations, fighting other organizations that try to do what their agency does, resisting new tasks that don't mesh with organizational capabilities or that involve divided constituencies, and steering clear of cooperative or joint ventures.[9] Autonomy results from careful management of the environment.

Some agencies possess particularly high levels of autonomy. As discussed in Chapter 2, the Federal Reserve Board (the Fed) enjoys a great deal of autonomy due in large part to its expertise in managing the economy through its manipulation of the money supply and its supervision of state-chartered banks that belong to the federal reserve system. A strong economy and healthy banking industry is a good indication of the Board's success in using its expertise. Even in times of economic crisis (or especially in times of economic crisis), the Fed's expert clout remains strong. Similarly, with a solvent bank insurance fund, the Federal

Deposit Insurance Corporation (FDIC) has typically enjoyed relative autonomy to manage bank failures and to supervise thousands of small, state-chartered banks that do not belong to the Federal Reserve system. A solvent fund is a simple, clear indicator that the agency is performing its task of maintaining confidence in the banking system. The black and gold "FDIC Insured" sticker on the window of every bank is a symbol of public reliance on a popular program charged with protecting the public's savings. In contrast, the Office of the Comptroller of the Currency (OCC), a bureau located within the Department of the Treasury, suffers a vague mandate and competition for its expertise. While both the Fed and the FDIC conduct tasks other than banking supervision (the Fed manages the money supply and the FDIC manages the Bank Insurance Fund), the OCC is strictly a supervisor of national banks. However, it is not clear from the OCC's mandate how, or to what ends, the OCC is to supervise banks. Its mandate to insure a "safe and sound" banking system has been interpreted in a variety of ways over the years. It has promoted greater risk taking and competition among banks, but it has also encouraged and enforced caution and conservative banking practices.[10] Such disparate messages have drawn the ire of members of Congress, its partners in regulation (the Fed and FDIC), and segments of the divided banking industry.

Public programs with a large degree of autonomy are likely to have more flexibility in making and maintaining changes in culture. After all, if the political environment is less of a factor, a leader can tend primarily to the definition of task and the application of resources and personnel if they want to make changes. With a less volatile environment, personnel (particularly professional personnel) and the nature of the task will play a dominant role in defining the way work is done. Such is the case at the Fed and the FDIC. Federal Reserve Board commitments to a reasonable regulatory approach and to respect for the expertise of its employees reflect the delicate nature of the central bank task, as well as the dominant influence of professional economists and bankers within the agency. A reasonable regulatory decision is one made with solid information and forecasts, and one that does not dramatically change past policy. Employees of the Fed emphasize that decisions are not influenced by the current political winds, but are based upon the best information and professional judgment the Board can bring to bear on any given issue.[11]

Similarly, the FDIC's commitments to protecting the fund, to workable solutions, and to conservative regulation and supervision reflect the dominant task of managing the fund and the influence of professional FDIC supervisors and examiners. Protecting the fund is the blood and guts of the FDIC task. All else grows from this identification. How the agency resolves a failed bank, how it supervises banks, and how it trains employees to do both (resolve banks and supervise banks) grow from this basic commitment to protect the fund. Conservative supervision has long been viewed a means to keeping banks healthy and free from the need of a bank fund bailout, although not necessarily to keeping them highly competitive and growing. Workable solutions for failures and supervisory problems reflect the professionalism of supervisors and examiners (working face to face with banks on a daily basis) concerned about keeping banks healthy without strangling them in a net of regulations.[12]

Yet neither the FDIC nor the Fed would have the luxury of finding ways to do their work in relatively autonomous environments if they did not do their tasks well, or if the constituencies they serve and impact were particularly unhappy with their regulatory efforts. Both agencies must attend to the integration of task, resources, and environment to maintain an autonomous situation. Fed chairman Alan Greenspan's ever-so-careful shepherding of economic information before congressional committees is testimony to the importance of working with the political environment to maintain Fed autonomy. The congressional, media, and public attention to his every word and every adjective describing the state of the economy serves to heighten the image of the Fed as the ultimate expert on the country's economic concerns. Should Greenspan or another Fed chair make definitive, partisan, or highly controversial presentations to Congress, the level of respect for Fed expertise might begin to erode. For the Fed, the exercise of reasonable regulation and a devotion to expertise not only reflect the integration of resources and the nature of the task, but the essential strategy to maintain autonomy by managing or working with the immediate environment.

In the late 1980s the FDIC experienced a serious threat to its autonomy, brought on by a crisis in the environment: banks and savings and loans began failing at a record rate and required huge bailouts. In its annual report in 1984, the FDIC boasted that public confidence had been maintained in the banking system for fifty years "without one penny of taxpayer money," and the bank insurance fund, funded through premiums paid by banks, was at an all-time high of $15 billion. By the close of the decade, however, after more than one thousand banks failed, the fund was projecting a $7 billion deficit and was authorized to borrow $30 billion from the Treasury Department to meet its obligations. The autonomy of the FDIC was shattered. Passage of the Financial Institutions Recovery Reform and Enforcement Act (FIRREA) of 1989—aimed at resolving failed savings and loans, with the help of the FDIC—and the Federal Deposit Insurance Corporation Improvement Act (FDICIA) injected congressional influence over FDIC supervisory and resolution activities for the first time. FDIC employees were not pleased. A division director commented on the impact of the legislation:

> [We have always] been opposed to attempts to minimize the discretion of an independent agency. . . . With FIRREA and FDICIA they began to micromanage us, not directly, but by telling the agency how to micromanage the industry . . . limiting our discretion.[13]

Efforts to regain that discretion required aggressive management of the ways in which the environment, task, and resources were fitting together at that point in time. Autonomy rested with the success of the FDIC in doing its task—protection of the fund through conservative supervision and workable solutions. But the political environment was foisting new definitions of "workable" solutions and "conservative" supervision on the agency. Without an effort to directly manage the integration of resources, task, and environment, the engrained commitments guiding the way work was done would gradually be altered, perhaps emphasizing supervision by explicit legislative mandate—that is, by the book. First, to reduce external scrutiny of its efforts to manage the banking crisis, the agency built its own internal capacity to handle more legal matters in house rather than depend upon a host of legal partners. Criticism not only of the extent to which the agency was relying upon external law firms, but of the conduct of investigations and cases by those firms, was one source of scrutiny that the agency hoped to eliminate by beefing up its own legal office. Second, the agency stepped up efforts to minimize conflict among consumer groups and members of Congress irritated by the agency's supervision of banks on issues of fairness and openness in lending. A new Office of Consumer Affairs was established, and the FDIC hired many Fed-trained examiners specializing in fair lending and consumer issues to fill its own ranks. The FDIC built a new training center in Virginia—a veritable campus devoted to the rigorous and continuous training of supervisors responsible for safe and sound banking. The move not only enhanced the quality and quantity of training for FDIC personnel, but it also created more opportunities for the agency to reinforce the importance of protecting the fund through conservative supervision and workable solutions. And while FDIC leadership attended to the external and broad managerial concerns of the agency to restore autonomy in its environment, regional- and district-level leaders sought to protect their supervisors from the onslaught of environmental pressures to ensure their professional supervisory efforts.

The commitments defining the work of the FDIC and the Fed reflect a careful balance of task, resources, and the environment that has been consistently maintained for decades. The maintenance of autonomy, in and of itself, is evidence of the importance Fed and FDIC leaders have placed upon managing the integration of task and resources with potentially volatile environments. To set out to change the commitments defining work in either agency would no doubt entail the destabilization, if not obliteration, of the autonomy enjoyed by both agencies. While autonomy might be an essential and valued quality of such agencies, it is important to remember that it is not necessarily valuable in and of itself. As the economy and the needs of the public change, leaders might view the tasks of the Fed and the FDIC in very different terms. A public manager who understands the meaning of a "safe and sound" banking system to be intensely competitive might work to change the commitment of the FDIC from one of conservative supervision to one of cooperative supervision, giving banks greater leeway to spread their lending wings. Such a task might require engaging the environment in different, perhaps more combative terms; redefining the task; and rethinking the resources, training, and personnel used to accomplish the task.

While a volatile environment might have obvious implications for the way the job gets done in a public program, the influence of a less volatile or even placid setting might be more difficult to connect to the commitments of a program. The manager who digs deep enough, however, will see the intricate and important connections between environmental autonomy (or the environment more generally) and the commitments that define the way the job gets done in a public program.

GETTING AT THE ROOTS OF CULTURE: THE SOUTH AFRICAN POLICE SERVICE

Herbert Kaufman's study of six federal bureau chiefs offers little promise about the ability of top-level public managers to bring about change in the programs they manage.[14] Leadership efforts are inevitably overshadowed by dominant factors in the environment and by the dynamics of large organizations. Congressional resistance stymies changes that might alter the influence of a committee on Capitol Hill or the influence of an individual member or his or her constituency. Executive branch efforts to centrally coordinate and influence the management of individual bureaus can seriously impede change. Interest groups stand ready to oppose changes that might impact their influence or benefits, and organized labor unions resist changes that threaten job security and pay. Organizations are linked with numerous other organizations, within government and without. Career staff, too, are linked to members of Congress and enjoy job security that promotes a "sit tight" attitude toward change—wait a year and the leadership will change. And learned routines and written rules and procedures further constrain the ability of a leader to make change. The task of change is nothing short of monumental. Leaders might be able to "set the tone" of the organization, "nudge" agendas, and build agency "prestige." Otherwise, their influence is limited.[15]

Yet the three cases illustrated in the previous chapter suggest that change in program culture is possible through the aggressive management of many of these constraining factors. The difference between achieving and not achieving change might rest with the size and age of a program, or with its complexity. Perhaps programs small in scale and with little history behind them are most amenable to change, or perhaps those evidencing little complexity. While this may make sense to us, we already know that this is not the case. FEMA is a large agency with a more than twenty-year history, responsible for a $937 million annual budget (FY 2001). And finding ways to stabilize and rebuild inner city neighborhoods is surely one of the most intransigent public policy problems in America. Yet ESLARP stands as a stellar example in a sea of failed public policy initiatives aimed at urban renewal. Similarly, violent crime and its psychological and social repercussions is an extremely complex public policy issue, but the partnership in New Haven between police and mental health professionals is finding ways to address the problem built around a commitment to finding community solutions for kids exposed to violence.

What might the crucial difference really be? In all of the cases discussed in Chapter 3, leaders took control of programs that were in a condition of crisis, where to many participants change was perceived both publicly and politically as essential. In 1993, before James Lee Witt took charge, FEMA was considered to be at the bottom of the unrecoverable bureaucratic heap. Prior to Kenneth Reardon's arrival, residents of East St. Louis bore the burden of a city in desperate financial distress, unable even to collect garbage let alone promote the local economy. And in 1991 the murder rate in New Haven, Connecticut, peaked at its highest point in the city's history, and gang warfare and drugs were commonplace in its middle and high schools. Simply put, the bureau chiefs in Kaufman's study, who were frustrated by their inability to bring about change, were not faced with conditions of crises anywhere near like those at FEMA and in East St. Louis and New Haven.

That said, it is important to realize that even under conditions of crisis, the task of changing a culture deeply embedded in a political and social environment that has shaped the definition of the task and the available resources can border on the impossible. Stephen Vukile Tshwete, who was appointed minister of safety and security in South Africa in June 1999, faced the monumental task of completely overhauling the concept and understanding of the way South African society is policed.[16]

Prior to 1990, when President F. W. de Klerk began to loosen the grip of apartheid in South Africa and lifted the ban on the African National Congress (ANC), the traditional South African Police Service (SAPS) focused on enforcing and protecting the apartheid regime. The police were militant, and use of maximum force first was its accepted response to the nation's black citizenry. The violent and unequal treatment of citizens by police was mirrored within the Police Service itself. In the early 1990s more than 60 percent of the police force was black, yet more than 95 percent of the officer corps was white. Even within the same rank or position, dramatic pay differences were in place between black and white police personnel, as well as differences in the quality and quantity of training afforded individual officers. Black police officers were typically deployed to the most turbulent and dangerous areas to fight unrest. Not surprisingly, they suffered the greatest number of deaths on the job.[17] Often confused with the South African Defense Force (the South African military), the Police Service pursued its mission to police civil unrest with a very militant approach. New recruits were trained not only in law enforcement and criminal investigation, but also in weaponry and hand-to-hand combat.[18] White officers on the force were largely Afrikaner men who joined SAPS to "defend white civilization."[19] The South

African Police Service, in short, was defined by a commitment to intense racism in the hiring, training, compensation, and promotion of police officers and in the enforcement of laws and to a commitment to militaristic policies and engagement when training recruits and enforcing the laws of apartheid.

Beginning in 1990, when President de Klerk initiated the transition to a new government—and eventually a new constitution in 1994—all forms of crime increased steadily in South Africa, but violent crime increased dramatically.[20] The problem continues to escalate today, and with such high crime rates have come sinking public expectations for police performance and even greater mistrust of the police. From 1994 to 1999 Tshwete's predecessor, Sydney Mufamadi, tried to tackle both the rising crime rate and the growing public mistrust by building partnerships between the police and local communities, particularly the black communities loyal to the ANC that feared and despised the police service. By 1997 more than one thousand community police forums (CPFs) had been established to create links between the police and local communities and to confer greater legitimacy on the police service in the eyes of the public. Numerous publications, including the SAPS handbook, promote the concept of a safer and more livable South Africa through community policing, which is presented as a shared responsibility between the police and community.[21] And consultants from across the globe have descended upon South Africa to offer expertise, training, and resources to build a community-based approach to policing. The abundance of international consultations and recommendations are a valuable resource for a country struggling to police a society framed by apartheid legacies and nascent democratic institutions.

Yet amid this abundance of community "links" and external resources aimed at transformation are numerous barriers. The roots of SAPS's traditional culture run very deep and might be beyond the immediate influence of any one leader. First, the environment poses a considerable obstacle. The militant and racist culture of SAPS grew out of a political regime that expected and supported the brutal enforcement of apartheid. Racism within SAPS became an extension of this political setting. Increasingly violent confrontations between black South Africans and SAPS, particularly throughout the 1980s, increased the levels of mistrust between the two and reinforced SAPS's militant efforts. They also led to the creation of two additional policing units, the Kitskonstabels (instant constables) and Greenflies (municipal police with green uniforms). These groups consisted primarily of unemployed black men hired from the rural areas of South Africa, members of vigilante groups, or supporters of the Zulu-based Inkatha movement that was fiercely opposed to the ANC.[22] Recruits were given minimal training and pay and expected to quell civil unrest and protect publicly unpopular municipal councils established to legitimize apartheid rule. Their inexperience and poor training only led to more violent confrontations and greater mistrust on the part of the public.[23]

Some scholars have argued that it is precisely the nascent nature of democratic and social institutions after apartheid that prevents the transformation of SAPS. Community policing requires strong communities and community organizations willing to participate and cooperate with the police in fighting crime. While the CPFs are a step in the right direction, they alone are not enough.[24] And they are not meant to be vehicles for controlling the police at the local level, as some CPF members have attempted. Such a use runs counter to the notion of cooperation and heightens the distrust between the police and the community.[25] Distrust is also heightened by the fact that, under apartheid, the police played a key role in trying to destroy the very communities now called upon to be its partners in the policing effort. The apartheid legacy limits the capacity of these communities to participate.[26] Indeed, one might argue that these communities must be made safe through rigorous policing of crime before a community-based approach can take root. Differences between white and black community preferences for community-based policing reflect this concern. Affluent whites are more supportive of community-based approaches to crime than are blacks in poorer areas, who tend to favor more aggressive policing to make their neighborhoods safe.[27]

A second significant obstacle to the success of Tshwete's efforts to change the culture of SAPS involves its internal resources (primarily personnel) and its traditional task. Before the new constitution went into effect in 1994, ten homeland police districts operated under varying degrees of direction from SAPS. These forces were staffed by indigenous people who were either transferred from within SAPS to a particular homeland police force or hired within the homelands themselves in order to maintain white supremacy and ethnic segregation both within SAPS and throughout South Africa as a whole.[28] The capacity and self-sufficiency of these forces varied significantly in terms of training and education, their degree of independence from SAPS and local political control, and the quality of police service afforded the public. SAPS often supported the promotion of officers considered "politically reliable" to avoid facilitating truly autonomous police forces. For many black officers, promotion and positions of authority not available in SAPS were more readily had in the segregated homelands. Yet without sufficient training and with only minimal authority to define policing procedures, corruption defined the work of many of the homeland forces. In some of the homelands, local headmen or tribal chiefs reportedly exercised significant influence over the police force, using it to harass political opponents, protect themselves, and provide jobs for family, friends, and supporters.[29] For local police officers who want to develop a more professional and independent force, particularly as the government of South Africa continues to undergo dramatic change, the situation is very frustrating. These semi-independent policing units were reincorporated back into SAPS following the change in government in order to facilitate reform and centralize the work of the police. But the varied experiences, training, and political affiliations of these forces present an enormous challenge to bringing about a new SAPS.

Other significant resource challenges remain as well. While outside consultants from across the globe have developed policy directives aimed at making SAPS a community-oriented police service, they rarely have an understanding or knowledge of the dynamics, resources, and constraints of the organization itself. Their recommendations simply fall through the cracks. Before it can put any "expert" recommendations into play, SAPS must hire, train, and promote officers skilled in fighting crime rather than fighting civil unrest. The organization must also develop a core of skilled managers trained not necessarily in strategic management and policy development, but in policing crime.[30] The effort to "legitimize" SAPS in the eyes of the public requires a return to the basics of policing—basics that could be the key to success for reform.[31]

We have highlighted the significant obstacles to a change in culture at SAPS. It is important to point out, however, that there are elements of the "roots" of culture that Minister Tshwete might be able to build upon to effect change. For example, a 1992 report on personnel noted a new generation of police officers anxious to be part of a more professional police service.[32] Tshwete might take advantage of such ambition and use it to build a more professional police service focused on the basics of good policing. In addition, Tshwete came to office with a pledge to improve both police resources and the conditions under which police officers work. Efforts to improve police training, oversight, and computer support are currently under way. Tshwete has focused on the immediate political environment by trying to build strong political support for tough policing, a position that was more difficult in the immediate aftermath of government transition and the violence perpetrated by SAPS. The minister has focused his energy not so much on the language and policies of community policing, but on rigorous policing of crime. In his first weeks in office Tshwete oversaw an aggressive anticrime campaign that included raids on scrap yards thought to service car thieves and the break up of a syndicate connected to a string of arsons.[33]

Tshwete's efforts to date have focused on key elements of the roots of SAPS's traditional culture. He has sought to alter the understanding of SAPS's task by focusing rigorously on fighting crime, and he has engaged his political overseers in efforts to support the same. He has worked to upgrade the resources and training his officers need to effectively fight crime, and has added to their capacity to gather information for tracking, investigating, and solving crimes. In short, he is offering officers alternatives to the old way of getting the job done and supporting his vision with resources and the necessary political clout. Nevertheless, the scope of the SAPS environment, from police departments to state departments to consulting firms across the globe, and the problems of public mistrust, rising crime, and nascent political and social institutions, combine to create a monumental environmental management challenge. A force traditionally segregated by training, promotion, pay, and deployment poses yet another impediment to change.

The task was apparently beyond the reach of Tshwete's predecessor, Minister Mufamadi, whose tenure was assessed as "little short of disasterous." In 1999 the Johannesburg Mail and Guardian reported that blacks within SAPS "complain bitterly of entrenched racism—and that nothing is being done about it."[34] Mufamadi issued numerous reports and conducted strategic planning sessions, but rising crime rates and continued public mistrust of the police left little doubt that SAPS's traditional culture remained deeply entrenched. Without clear alternatives to the way work has historically been done, SAPS's traditional culture might linger for years to come. Tshwete appears to be taking smaller but more incisive bites at the roots of culture. Whether or not he succeeds in effecting real change, replacing traditional commitments with new ones, remains to be seen.

And what if Minister Tshwete does succeed in changing the commitments that define the way work is done in SAPS? Will the changes stick when he is no longer minister of safety and security?

MAKING CHANGES STICK

A persistent manager of a public program will continuously work at the roots of culture to find ways to change or build program commitments that facilitate a vision or an understanding of the way the job should get done. The creative manager will find ways to weave emerging commitments into the institutional routines of a public program. In the previous chapter, we saw that the managers of ESLARP, FEMA, and the CD–CP mental health partnership used employee training, course offerings in the university curriculum, routine or annual summits or retreats, regular customer surveys, and offices or seminars that physically connected program partners as ways to facilitate and engrain changes in program commitments. But the ability of change to stick seems to rest upon a combination of a leader's efforts to continuously manage the roots of culture toward a particular end and the integration of the resulting changes into program structure and routines. Some organizations, such as the South African Police Service, have deep cultural roots with commitments intricately wound through every dimension of the program. Without continuing aggressive efforts to manage the roots of culture the traditional culture is likely to stay in place or take hold once again when a leader departs.

An example of a deeply engrained culture that reemerged after aggressive efforts by a leader to change it is the culture of the Securities and Exchange Commission (SEC). James Landis led the SEC in its formative years.[35] He defined the task of the SEC as regulation of the securities markets through full public disclosure of publicly traded companies and rigorous enforcement of securities laws. He demurred a bit in the exercise of the SEC's rulemaking power to regulate trading and activities in the securities markets. Landis hired and supported attorneys who shared his views of the SEC's mission, and he worked to build support for his approach on Wall Street and in Congress. In short, he managed the integration of task, resources, and environment to facilitate his objectives. Landis's approach was institutionalized in SEC procedures, division structure, and personnel practices. In 1983 the newly appointed chairman, John Shad, challenged the culture of the SEC. Shad sought to redefine the task of the SEC to one of facilitating the flow of capital by reducing the burden of disclosure for publicly traded companies. He directly challenged the personnel and resources brought to bear on the work of the SEC by creating the Office of the Chief Economist and hiring economists with Ph.D.s, training, and publications in free-market theories. Shad was never completely successful in managing the environment necessary to support such a vision, in large part because many in Congress with SEC oversight were not convinced of the necessity of the changes—indeed, they saw the changes as subversive to the interests of individual investors. When Shad left the SEC, the dominant commitments to disclosure and enforcement took hold once again. An environment, particularly the Congress, long supportive of a particular approach to regulating the markets, a securities industry similarly supportive, and personnel trained in securities law all integrate to maintain a culture built on legal remedies and disclosure enforcement.

As the example of the SEC illustrates, a leader trying to change culture must try to make new commitments part of the routine of the program by creating new offices, hiring new personnel, retraining existing personnel, and creating forums or opportunities for alternative forms of participation. But while changes in structure, personnel, and procedure are necessary to maintain culture change, they alone will not suffice. A leader must continuously manage the roots of culture toward a particular end as well. Consider efforts by university presidents across the country to alter the culture of engagement between labor unions on campus (including faculty unions) and administration. The goal in many cases is to replace commitments to formal engagement, litigation, and lack of trust with commitments to collaboration and inclusive decision making. A delicate balance exists between the university president committed to change and the institutional framework for collaboration and inclusion. To effect change university presidents can redefine the partnership between unions and administration by extending power to the former—making unions a part of key decision-making efforts. This not only redefines the task and the nature of the relationship between unions and administration but alters the mix of personnel, resources, and ideas involved in key decision-making efforts. The president of a large public university in the Midwest regularly hosts dinners with members of the organized faculty union and faculty senate to deal with matters such as parking, voting rights for faculty with joint appointments, and improved faculty recreation facilities. This removes many conflicts for broader negotiations and simultaneously builds trust and better communication between the faculty union and the president.[36] Others talk of open door policies, presidential leadership councils, and other forums for making the gap between administration and organized work forces "seamless." But it is precisely the creation of such forums that makes the president integral to at least half of the effort to create and maintain collaborative settings. One university administrator described the necessary balance between an individual leader working to create a certain kind of culture and the frameworks created to support collaboration and inclusion:

> There are methods, processes in place that help foster the collaborative approach. They work hard on the relationship, too, but there are times when participants just don't have time for the information sharing, getting to know each other. . . . Sometimes people just don't trust each other. Or there is a strong initial fear about working in a collaborative manner. Then it's good to have a system in place that forces the process. People might be interested, but they just don't know how to start. At the same time, the system will fail if the people are not committed to the process.[37]

The ability of culture to stick depends significantly upon the efforts of a public manager as leader. If she or he views the integration of task, resources, and environment as a central and ongoing management responsibility, then she or he has the potential to alter the roots of culture in ways that alter program commitments—that is, in the way the job gets done. Any changes must then be institutionalized through use and repetition and—eventually—through the acceptance by program employees of the relevance and importance of a process, approach, office, or organizational scheme. But change hinges too on the structures that the public manager both influences and operates within. In a self-deprecating manner, Kenneth Reardon noted, "The lead faculty member colors the approach."[38] Today, ESLARP's continuing commitment to shared responsibility rests with the approach and understanding of the lead faculty member who replaced Reardon in 2000.

CONCLUSION

The cultural roots model focuses on managing culture by managing the way the roots of culture weave together. The questions raised in this chapter and the examples presented highlight the utility of the model's use of commitments to capture the essence of culture, and the importance of the environment as a key root of culture requiring management. The questions raised and examples presented also suggest ways the model can be extended to address the manageability of particularly durable roots and the legacy of culture change when a leader departs.

First, the cultural roots model focuses on program commitments rather than on a more elaborate portrayal of culture. The first question we posed at the beginning of this chapter was whether commitments can capture the essence of culture. If the intent of trying to manage culture is to change the way the job gets done, an emphasis on commitments seems appropriate. The identification of a commitment might not allow for more nuanced differences in the beliefs and basic assumptions of participants in a public program. And the identification of a commitment might not reveal divergent understandings of the work held by some participants in the program, or variations in the depth with which the commitments are held. But the identification of a commitment offers insight into the way the job gets done in a public program and why. If a manager is able to identify a commitment and can connect the commitment to the integration of cultural roots, the manager can begin to see what needs management attention if the job is to be done differently.

Second, the cultural roots model includes the environment as a key element of culture. The second question we posed was whether the environment is always a factor, particularly for those public programs that seem to operate autonomously within the political world. As the examples of federal banking agencies suggest, attention to the environment by top managers is essential for maintaining some autonomy, and hence for the commitments that have evolved. The commitments of the Fed and the FDIC reflect the priorities of professional personnel in both agencies and the nature of the tasks they perform, but maintenance of these commitments requires careful attention to the environment within which they operate. When legislators were alarmed by dramatic losses in the bank insurance fund in the 1980s, for example, the autonomous environment of the FDIC was temporarily shattered and its key commitments challenged. Careful attention to the concerns of lawmakers and to the FDIC's management of the fund, however, restored much of the institution's original autonomy and helped to maintain commitments that had evolved over more than sixty years.

Finally, the third and fourth questions we posed at the beginning of this chapter introduce discussion of the ways in which we may extend the cultural roots model. We saw that Stephen Vukile Tshwete, as minister of safety and security in South Africa, faces a considerable challenge in managing the roots of SAPS culture, which are both deep and complex. While Tshwete's post-apartheid predecessor was unsuccessful at effecting change, Tshwete has at least begun engaging the roots of SAPS culture, trying to redefine the nature of the task before SAPS personnel and providing the resources to support that redefinition. Just as important, he has engaged the political environment to build support for the new approach, rather than allowing the vast number of participants in SAPS's global environment to define the task and resources for him.

While there are indications that his efforts to shake loose the commitments established under apartheid are working, the fourth question we posed at the beginning of this chapter asks whether any changes Tshwete is able to make to SAPS's culture will endure after he leaves office. When the tenure of a public manager who has aggressively managed the roots of culture comes to an end, will the changes he or she made stick? The cultural roots model presents a mix of leadership, environment, task, and resources as a means to understand the commitments of a program culture. How the roots of culture are integrated depends largely on the program leader. Leaders can try to change the process of integration and build those changes into the program through structural, personnel, and procedural changes. But institutional changes alone do not keep new commitments in place. Management of the roots of culture is a constant endeavor, and leaders who choose to continue a process of integration established in a program's formative years will likely preside over a traditional culture, as in the case of SEC leaders before and after John Shad. Similarly, efforts to change the cultural commitments defining the way the job gets done on university campuses involving administration and unions require a mix of leadership and the creation of alternative structures or procedures in which to pursue collaboration and more inclusive decision making. A leader's legacy of collaboration and inclusion might linger in an organization, but the commitments won't persevere unless the next leader similarly turns his or her attention to managing the roots of culture in a way that facilitates collaboration and inclusion.

Before cultural legacies are a consideration, however, a public manager must have the capacity to sense the big picture that is culture, and the connections between the cultural commitments and the roots of culture. For many leaders, this ability is instinctive. Indeed, the managers in Chapter 3 who changed program commitments might even find humorous the extraction of a "model" from practices they deem commonsense management of tough programs. But not all managers are successful in transforming program cultures, nor is an ability to view cultural commitments (the way the job gets done) a natural inclination for many trained and practiced in the trenches of public program implementation. In the following chapter we will examine one researcher's approach to the "soaking in and poking around" that is necessary to perceive culture and its roots.

Notes

1. Linda Smircich identifies several different ways to conceptualize culture, such as an "adaptive regulatory mechanism" incorporated by corporate culture researchers, a "system of shared cognitions," or a "projection of mind's universal unconscious infrastructure." It can also be conceptualized as a "root metaphor," shifting the researcher's focus "from concerns about what do organizations accomplish and how may they accomplish it more efficiently, to how is organization accomplished and what does it mean to be organized?" See Smircich, "Concepts of Culture and Organizational Analysis," *Administrative Science Quarterly* 28 (1983): 342.

2. Edgar Schein, *Organizational Culture and Leadership* (San Francisco: Jossey-Bass, 1985); and Schein, *Organizational Culture and Leadership,* 2d ed. (San Francisco: Jossey-Bass, 1990).

3. J. Steven Ott, *The Organizational Culture Perspective* (Pacific Grove, Calif.: Brooks/Cole, 1989), 62.

4. Steven Marans, in collaboration with Jean Adnopoz, Miriam Berkman, Dean Esserman, Douglas MacDonald, Steven Nagler, Richard Randall, Mark Schaefer, and Melvin Wearing, *The Police–Mental Health Partnership: A Community-Based Response to Urban Violence* (New Haven: Yale University Press, 1995), 108.

5. Ibid., 109.

6. Ibid., 109–111.

7. James Q. Wilson, *Bureaucracy: What Government Agencies Do and Why They Do It* (New York: Basic Books, 1989), 181–195.

8. See Francis Rourke, *Bureaucracy, Politics and Public Policy,* 3d ed. (Boston: Little, Brown, 1984), for a similar argument.

9. Wilson, *Bureaucracy,* 188–192.

10. Anne Khademian, *Checking on Banks: Autonomy and Accountability in Three Federal Agencies* (Washington, D.C.: Brookings, 1996), 85–112.

11. Ibid., 136–142.

12. Ibid., 116–127.

13. Quoted in ibid., 117.

14. Herbert Kaufman, *The Administrative Behavior of Federal Bureau Chiefs* (Washington, D.C.: Brookings, 1981).

15. Ibid., 139–174.

16. Mark Malan, "Police Reform in South Africa: Peacebuilding without the Peacekeepers." This article was published in support of Training for Peace, a project sponsored by the government of Norway and executed by the Institute for Security Studies in partnership with the Norwegian Institute for International Affairs and the African Centre for the Constructive Resolution of Disputes. It borrows from Malan, "Peacebuilding in Southern Africa: Police Reform in Mozambique and South Africa" (paper presented at the Conference on International Support for Police Reform in Transitions from War to Peace, Oslo, March 5–6, 1999). Retrieved from the Web, February 2001, at http://www.iss.co.za/Pubs/ASR/8.3/.

17. Janine Rauch, "State, Civil Society and Police Reform in South Africa" (paper presented at the International Society of Criminology conference, Budapest, Hungary, August 1993). Retrieved from the Web, February 2001, at http://www.iss.co.za/Pubs/ASR/8.3/Police%20reform.html.

18. Esther Scott, "Changing with the Times: The South African Police in the Post-Apartheid Era," Case Program, Kennedy School of Government, Harvard University, 1991, 3.

19. Ibid.

20. Malan, "Police Reform in South Africa."

21. Ibid.

22. Scott, "Changing with the Times," 9.

23. Ibid., 10.

24. Malan, "Police Reform in South Africa."

25. Ibid.

26. Rauch, "State, Civil Society and Police Reform."

27. Malan, "Police Reform in South Africa." See Antoinette Louw & Mark Shaw, *Stolen Opportunities: The Impact of Crime on South Africa's Poor,* ISS Monograph Series, vol. 14, (Pretoria: Institute for Security Studies, Halfway House, July 1997).

28. Etienne Marais, "Policing the Periphery: Police and Society in South African's Home Land"(paper presented at the 22nd Congress of the Association for Sociology in South Africa, Pretoria, June 30, 1992).

29. Ibid.

30. Malan, "Police Reform in South Africa."

31. Ibid.

32. Marais, "Policing the Periphery."

33. "Morale-Boosting Plan Seems to Be Working," *Sowetan,* August 12, 1999. Retrieved from the Web, January 2001, at http://www.docuweb.ca/SouthAfrica/news/990816.html.

34. "Thabo Mbeki's First Cabinet: From the A to Z of South African Politics," *Daily Mail and Guardian,* June 18, 1999. Retrieved from the Web, November 2001, at http://www.mg.co.za/mg/za/news/99jun/cabinet/mufamadi.html.

35. The material in this discussion is based upon Anne Khademian, *The SEC and Capital Market Regulation: The Politics of Expertise* (Pittsburgh: University of Pittsburgh Press, 1992).

36. Elson Floyd, telephone interview with the author, December 21, 1998.

37. Scott Hill-Kennedy, telephone interview with the author, November 18, 1998.

38. Kenneth Reardon, telephone interview with the author, November 3, 2000.

C h a p t e r

5

Detecting Cultural
Commitments
An Exercise

IN CHAPTER 3 WE BORROWED RICHARD FENNO'S PHRASE "soaking and poking—or just hanging around" to describe the method managers
might use to detect the cultural commitments of a program and their connections to cultural roots.[1] Fenno's method applies to the work of a researcher who
goes into the field to explore a particular phenomenon or find answers to a specific question. She or he gathers information, makes observations, soaks up the
setting, and pokes around at the phenomenon, asking additional questions. As
responses to questions, observations, and other information are gathered, the researcher sorts, thinks, and analyzes—and then sorts some more, looking for patterns shaped by a preponderance of data. Tentative explanations emerge. The researcher tests these explanations against other sources of data, published
information, and additional findings. He or she expands the database to do more
soaking up and more poking around before taking another crack at an explanation. The more formal term for this method of research is "participant observation."[2] The researcher is in the field to observe a particular phenomenon first-
hand, but his or her presence makes the researcher something of a participant as
well.

Public managers attempting to manage the roots of program culture are also
participant observers. They are deeply engaged with employees and partners on a
day-to-day basis to ensure the job gets done. But they are also observers, able to
detach themselves from the daily minutia of organization efforts to observe the
way work is done and the ways in which commitments are manifest in a variety of
organization details. Their "research" begins with a two-part question: "What
commitments define the way work is done in the program, and how do these
commitments connect to the roots of culture?" They then embark on the "soaking
and poking" that will provide them with answers to this question by absorbing

details of program life and the surrounding environment to identify patterns, symbols, forms of communication, and attitudes and behavior toward the outside world that together suggest organizational commitments.

This chapter offers the manager some practical guidance to "soaking and poking" through program cultures to detect cultural commitments. It is unrealistic to assume that a manager has the time of a researcher conducting participant observation to investigate the dimensions of program culture. Social scientists sometimes devote years to the investigation of a single question. But the model of participant observation can serve as a guide for managerial efforts. The managers in Chapter 3 were able to rework the roots of program cultures in part because they began their tenures as good observers. While the demands on their time did not allow for the depth of observation similar to that undertaken by a researcher in the field, they each were good listeners and learners and used both skills to gather information and construct a map of the existing culture. Detecting and understanding the existing commitments is essential before a manager can pursue change by reworking the roots of culture. Describing his approach to leadership, James Lee Witt said, "You have to try to be open, honest, straightforward, and listen. We have to learn to do more listening."[3] Witt listened to employees in the morning by the elevators, he listened every Tuesday morning in his office, and every day while walking around the agency he listened. Witt listened to FEMA partners in meetings, at the site of disasters, in training and disaster preparedness settings, and daily on the phone or while traveling throughout the country. And Witt used the information he gathered from listening to learn—to inform, update, and modify his initial ideas about the agency and to think about ways to improve communication and better serve FEMA's customers.

Our focus in this chapter is on ways to detect an existing culture. To do this we must produce a map of program commitments that are in place and the connections of each commitment to the environment, resources, and task at hand. In the following chapter we will refer to the case studies in Chapter 3 to examine leadership styles that have been successful in uprooting and then rerooting program cultures. The program managers at ESLARP, FEMA, and the CD–CP mental health partnership successfully changed their respective program's culture after detecting and then altering existing cultural commitments. In essence, Kenneth Reardon, James Witt, and Nicholas Pastore listened and learned in order to construct a map of existing commitments and the connections between those commitments and cultural roots to effect real change in the programs for which they were responsible.

GETTING A CLEAR PICTURE

Managers can begin by getting a clear picture of the roots of program culture—in other words, by identifying the program task, the resources, and the personnel involved in the work of the program and understanding the environment surrounding the program. As with the researcher in the field, this requires listening and observing, and learning from what is heard and seen to update or adjust initial perceptions and assumptions.

The Task

First, a manager should think about the primary task or tasks of the program. This step can have three dimensions. The first dimension is the way participants (employees) in the program understand the task. The second is the way those outside the program (the public, organized groups, politicians) and those who are served by the program understand the task. And the third dimension is the way the public manager understands the task and the ways that he or she might want to change or redefine the task. When Professor Reardon assumed responsibility for UEMAP, participants within the university understood the task to be the application of faculty expertise to conduct research and develop designs aimed at stabilizing and improving life in East St. Louis. Under this definition of the task, residents of East St. Louis were outsiders. By listening to the residents in his initial interviews, Reardon learned their understanding of the program: Specifically, they saw it as another in a long line of programs targeting poor cities but disconnected from the residents. Reardon himself held a vision of the task that combined university expertise with the knowledge and experience of residents to build a partnership approach to stabilizing and revitalizing East St. Louis.

As the manager works through various definitions or understandings of the task, it is necessary to consider why the program was created in the first place and to ascertain whether or not participants or political overseers have ever attached a clear mission or sense of responsibility to the program. Public managers are not free to re-create programs. They operate within a system of accountability defined first and foremost by program mandates. The legislative debates and final mandate provide a continuous guide to public managers and employees working within public programs.[4] Managers do have flexibility, but that flexibility comes only through attention to the political constraints that defined the program initially, and careful attention to the concerns of political overseers, members of the public, and clients served by the program as changes in culture are undertaken.

In the case of UEMAP, the intent of the state legislature—or at least of state representative Wyvetter Younge, chairwoman of the committee responsible for University of Illinois funding and resident of East St. Louis—was for the university to apply its vast expertise to help stabilize and guide redevelopment of East St. Louis. The program's title, Urban Extension and Minority Access Project, suggested a partnership with, or at least a role for, East St. Louis residents. Reardon's participatory research approach certainly fit within these restrictions, as did the establishment of the Neighborhood College, which provided access to university resources. As the definition of the task evolved to include direct action organiz-ing, Reardon and other participants upped the ante for university overseers as well as politicians throughout the city of East St. Louis and the surrounding county. It was, however, an essential evolution from the perspective of residents as both participants in the program and those directly affected by the success or fail-ure of the program. And it was an evolution guided by a willingness on the part of Reardon and other program participants to learn while they were listening to the way work was being conducted around them.

Resources and Personnel

Second, managers should identify the primary resources used to implement the program and the primary personnel involved in implementation. Public pro-grams by definition receive money from the government, but funding sources can be complex. Under UEMAP, funding was limited to university funds that origi-nally came from the state legislature. Under ESLARP, money came from a variety of sources, including university funding, grants from the federal government, money from the city of East St. Louis and from St. Clair County, and hundreds of thousands of dollars from private and public sources raised through neighbor-hood associations that were established as development corporations. Some pub-lic programs receive money from other public organizations, sometimes in the same government (local, state, or federal) and sometimes across federal bound-aries. Others generate income from fees for services or products. Each source of funding can create different pressures or expectations for the way that the work is done within a program. The manager attentive to these potentially diverse sets of expectations will be better informed about the possible connections between re-sources and program commitments.

Managers should also have an understanding of the personnel involved in im-plementing the public program. What professional or employee groups make up the workforce? Are there particular dimensions or characteristics of the profes-sions that stand out in the work of the program? Under UEMAP, the primary professional group was university professors trained as architects, urban and re-gional planners, and landscape architects. Their control over program identifica-tion and design was the most significant characteristic that defined the emphasis on academic expertise. When Reardon and his colleagues expanded the personnel mix to include residents and hundreds of students, the skills and experience nec-essary to participate changed dramatically. Within the university Reardon and his colleagues were attempting to redefine the professional roles and obligations of university faculty to directly grapple with and participate in the implementation of solutions for addressing economic and social decline. They were also con-fronting the ways in which faculty worked together, across disciplines, and to-ward what ends.[5]

Environment

Finally, in order to get a picture of the roots of program culture, a manager should try to comprehend the environment within which the program operates. This step might be more easily approached if the environment is broken down into its various dimensions: formal accountability, partners, competitors, customers, systems of meaning, and local and regional influences.

Formal Accountability. Managers first must identify the primary overseer of the program. Another way of attacking this is to ask, "Where does the authority to implement the program and the money to do so come from?" A city council? A congressional committee? A state legislative committee? Or perhaps a federal- or state-level agency administering a grant program? Managers must then identify other political figures with responsibility for the program, or formal authority to influence the program. For example, a chief executive officer such as a mayor or governor might be able to make personnel appointments to a program, or a central management office such as the federal Office of Management and Budget could set budgeting, personnel, and procurement standards. Finally, managers must identify agencies or offices utilized by politicians to oversee and investigate the work of the program. The General Accounting Office is dispatched by members of Congress to investigate, report, and make recommendations for improving public programs. A state legislative audit bureau plays a similar watchdog role, as can outside consulting firms hired by elected officials or grant administrators to investigate the progress of particular public programs.

Given all of these potential layers of formal oversight, a manager then must ask, "How is accountability pursued in each case? And what expectations do overseers have with respect to performance?" A mixture of formal and informal communications often drives this process, from testimony before a legislative body to formal reports or responses to individual legislative inquiries to discussions on the phone or in person.

Under UEMAP, the links of formal political oversight were twofold. First, the state legislature, particularly the appropriation committee responsible for funding the university, appropriated money to the university, which then established money for the program. The chairwoman of this committee had primary interest in the program. Second, once the money was appropriated to the university, the individual directors or chairs of Architecture, Landscape Architecture, and Urban and Regional Planning were responsible for allocating the money among faculty and receiving final projects or reports for the work. When the program became ESLARP, a faculty executive committee was created to review major project proposals. Funding was pooled in 1995, and faculty began reporting to the dean of the College of Fine and Applied Arts in 1998, rather than to the individual department chairs.[6] These changes in personnel and structures of accountability within the university were critical in promoting an interdisciplinary approach to the work of ESLARP, pulling the emphasis away from individual department chairs, and for supporting a participatory research approach that included students, residents, and faculty. Different expectations of how a program ought to be held accountable, and different systems for achieving accountability, matter a great deal for the way in which work within a public program is accomplished.

Partners. Managers need to ask, "What individuals, groups, or organizations serve as partners in implementing the program?" Partners might play a role in implementation of the program or provide key support for the program. Agencies in the same or different level of government, coalitions, professional organizations, community groups, businesses, nonprofit organizations, and unions are among possible partners in implementation. Partnerships can be formal, based upon contracts or mandated cooperation, or evolve in a more informal manner through referrals, shared resources, overlapping constituencies, or personal ties. As in the case of funding and oversight, each partner brings a unique set of expectations to the relationship that help to shape the integration of resources, task, and environment.

Prior to Kenneth Reardon's tenure, partners with UEMAP were limited. Faculty worked on individual projects and reported to individual departments. As UEMAP and eventually ESLARP evolved, partners multiplied, as did the number of expectations and priorities placed upon the program. East St. Louis residents held expectations for participation in the identification, research, and implementation of projects. Neighborhood organizations had expectations for building organizational capacity and growing to become nonprofit development corporations. The city government of East St. Louis had expectations for tapping supporters of the dominant political party for purposes of contracts, planning, and accounting. Students had expectations to participate fully and learn new approaches to urban renewal. Understanding such a diverse array of expectations is a crucial element for making connections between the environment and the way the job gets done.

Partners also take the form of political supporters working within government and with the public to promote and nurture the work of the program. Representative Younge partnered with UEMAP. Her insistence upon a university response to urban decline, as well as her continued interest and efforts to bring UEMAP programs to fruition, demonstrated her commitment. Her power as chair of the educational appropriations committee made her a potentially powerful partner— but one that had limited opportunity to help bring about change in East St. Louis with UEMAP.

Competitors. Distinguishing between partners and competitors can be tricky. For example, the three federal agencies responsible for supervising the state- and nationally chartered banks of the United States can operate as allies or antagonists, depending on one's perspective. On the one hand, the Federal Deposit

Insurance Corporation (FDIC), Office of the Comptroller of the Currency (OCC), and Federal Reserve system are partners. They must work together to resolve failing banks. A failing bank must be resolved (liquidated or sold and depositors protected) by the FDIC, but if the bank is a nationally chartered bank, or a state-chartered bank that belongs to the Federal Reserve system, either the OCC or the Federal Reserve system will play a role too. And if the failing bank is sold, either the Federal Reserve system or the OCC might supervise the acquiring bank. The three agencies must also work together to develop regulations and minimize differences. While each agency is responsible for supervising a particular type of bank—state-chartered banks (FDIC), nationally chartered banks (OCC), and state-chartered banks belonging to the Federal Reserve system— supervision of a bank bundled within a larger bank or bank holding company requires cooperation between the supervisors of each agency. On the other hand, efforts to consolidate supervision at the federal level create competition among the regulators for maintaining bank supervisory turf.[7]

Despite the confusion, it is useful for a public manager to identify competitors in the environment, or partners that can behave like and play the role of competitors. As with partners, it is useful to think of competitors both in terms of implementation and as players in the political arena. UEMAP, and eventually ESLARP, had a competitor in the form of the Cooperative Extension Service at the University of Illinois. Particularly as faculty and students became increasingly engaged with residents and neighborhood organizations in East St. Louis, Extension viewed ESLARP as a competitor in the provision of outreach, and at one time sought to make ESLARP part of the Extension Service. More than an issue of turf, the two programs clashed in terms of organization and approach to outreach. Extension's hierarchical system of organization and its emphasis on university expertise and minimal shared responsibility stood in direct contrast to ESLARP's decentralized organizational structure, shared power, and shared responsibility for urban renewal.[8]

Again, listening and learning to develop a sense of who or what competes with a program, and how, can offer the manager insight into a program's environment and the ways in which the environment weaves through the work of the program.

Customers. Who does a public program directly serve or influence? The exercise of identifying customers can be complex.[9] Some programs or organizations don't provide a service to the public directly, but assist other government agencies or elected officials. The federal Office of Personnel Management, for example, is the personnel arm of the presidency and establishes and enforces personnel policies for executive branch agencies. The General Accounting Office, on the other hand, provides evaluations and audits of programs for its primary customer, the Congress. Distance from any customer population or group also makes identification of a customer population problematic. Many federal programs sit atop a long chain of implementation that eventually reaches an actual customer served by program funds. Grant money may travel from the federal government to a state agency and finally to an organization contracting with a local government to provide social services.

The clarity or ease of identifying a customer population can be a significant environmental influence over the development of commitments in a public program. An actual program commitment to customer service, for example, is more likely in a public program with a very clear sense of who the customers are and what is to be done for the customers. The U.S. Mint in Denver, Colorado, has made dramatic changes in the way work is done, beginning with a commitment to customer service.[10] Part of the organization's success in this effort is the clarity with which the Mint could identify its customer base. The Federal Reserve system is the Mint's biggest customer, buying 20 billion coins annually for circulation in the economy. The Mint also has several million smaller customers who collect and invest in commemorative coins and special issue and bullion coins. And the Mint has the means to evaluate its performance by measuring the increase or decrease in profits generated from the sale of coins—an amount that is turned over to the U.S. Treasury each year.

A customer base that is less clear, or that presents an organization with conflicting customer demands and needs, can also have a significant impact on the development of program commitments. The OCC, for example, has a task that presents the agency with two, often conflicting, sets of customers—depositors and the nationally chartered banks. While the national banks typically seek ways to be more aggressive and competitive in the financial industry, the fluctuations of mergers and acquisitions and risk taking that can lead to failures can cut against depositor concerns for safety and soundness. The agency's mandate is vague with respect to the priority that should be given to one set of customers over the other. Efforts to measure agency success are often open to debate in the political arena. Should emphasis be given to the stability and soundness of financial institutions, or to the growth in income, size, and number of nationally chartered banks? These factors play a prominent role in the evolution of organizational commitments that define the work of the agency.[11]

How public managers identify customers, indeed whether they use the term "customers" at all, is critical to thinking about the environment and its impact on program culture. Where one public manager might see a customer who needs to be served, another might see a citizen with "ownership" of the government and therefore of the program.[12] Still another might see a partner who has a responsibility to bring the program to fruition. Consider the students participating in ESLARP. One might identify university students as customers of ESLARP who purchase university credits to participate in the learning opportunities of the program. But the term "customer" sets a tone of one-way responsibility—the program toward the customers (in this case the students). But if a manager envisions dual responsibility, such as in ESLARP, customers might be more readily identified as partners. This certainly would be a more accurate description of the role students played throughout the 1990s in ESLARP.

Systems of Meaning. Key components of any environment are the systems of meaning within which a public program is implemented. As discussed in Chapter 2, a system of meaning is a construction of ideas for understanding a process or phenomenon. A system of meaning with relevance for a public program could be very specific or very broad with significance for all public programs. For example, the practice of comparing the public to the private sector has been one way that citizens evaluate the work of public programs. Americans have long looked to business as a standard toward which the public sector should aim—creativity, responsiveness to leadership, attentiveness to the bottom line, and responsiveness to customers. The current emphasis on performance—defining it, measuring it, and using it to evaluate employees and budget for agencies—is representative of a system of meaning based in the business world but widely used as a benchmark for understanding change and successful performance in the public sector. Much of the current reform efforts at the local, state, and national levels of government represent ideas based in the system of meaning that guides our understanding of successful performance. Legislators draw upon this system of meaning to impose performance standards on government agencies across the board.[13] Executive branch leaders and top managers of organizations adopt performance ideas to bring about change in government programs.[14] And in some cases an emphasis on performance is integrated with the way the task is understood, expectations from the environment, and training of personnel; some government agencies, in other words, approach the job as if they were a private company.[15]

Systems of meaning can enable or constrain efforts by a public manager to change program commitments. A manager wanting to foster a commitment to customer service can draw upon an environment teaming with consultants, training material, literature, and other public and private managers to influence the way personnel are trained, the way the program task is defined, and the way the program interacts with other programs and the public. However, a public manager seeking to focus program energy less upon measurable outcomes and more upon the processes of engagement, and even creating a sense of responsibility among participants toward a process of engagement, will have less environmental capital to draw upon.[16]

Participants in ESLARP faced two constraining systems of meaning in their efforts to build a program based upon shared responsibility: a system of meaning based upon academic expertise that defined work within a university setting, and the broader system of meaning focused on performance and results as key to program success. While the former has been discussed at length, the latter requires some elaboration. Participants in ESLARP wanted, and still want, performance. They want safer and cleaner neighborhoods, economic growth, and new jobs. But achieving those results requires significant attention to procedure—how par-

DETECTING CULTURAL COMMITMENTS 117

ticipants engage with each other to plan, develop, build, and evaluate. Excessive attention to results prevents the essential focus on how to get to those results, and even to attend to the issues of what results residents want and how those priorities may change over time. Initially, UEMAP faculty members were focused on results. They designed and developed projects. But the projects didn't come to fruition. A system of meaning that pushes public programs to define results and get there quickly can limit the essential processes of figuring out what results are necessary, and getting there in a way that matters as much as the results themselves.

A manager needs to understand the systems of meaning surrounding a program and the implications for how participants interpret and approach the program task. The changes pursued by the manager may require engaging and even trying to change the relevant systems of meaning used by members of the public, political officials, partners, and program clientele to judge the program's value and effectiveness.

Local and Regional Influences. Just as systems of meaning provide context within which government programs are implemented, local or regional factors can be a significant environmental influence. Public managers can identify local or regional characteristics that might influence the training or work of employees, their approach to public service, or their understanding of the task at hand.

Every locality, region, or country has its own distinct way of doing things that seeps into the work of any given public program. One can sense differences between the FDIC field offices in Milwaukee and Dallas just by stepping into their offices. Each culture is reflected in the attitude of supervisors toward the banks they supervise, the décor of the offices, and in the sense of professional independence expressed by supervisors vis-à-vis the agency itself. A program or program unit based in a state with a strong progressive tradition and positive support for government will approach its work somewhat differently than a similar organization in a state with a strong tradition of independence from government and support for minimal government. Just how relevant some of these differences are, however, for the work of the program depends greatly upon the program. Despite differences in style between the FDIC field offices, an overriding commitment to protecting the fund and a conservative approach to supervision is present across field offices. A program with commitments that offer a strong guide and source of motivation can direct employees to the same approach, and through its training and reward process build loyalty to that approach. As with the FDIC, such a program might experience mild differences across regional offices or divisions.

IDENTIFYING COMMITMENTS

After a manager has identified the roots of culture, he or she must next investigate the way work is done in the program. Watching, asking questions, and listening are the best strategies for accomplishing this. Managers should observe the work from the top down—that is, from top management down to line personnel. They should listen to people in different divisions and offices and at partnering organizations, observing the daily work. If the organization is spread out geographically, they should compare and contrast their observations in different geographical settings. Does location matter? Are there local or regional differences?

Comparing experiences between current and former employees of the program can provide valuable information as well. Managers might seek out past leaders and previous employees of the organization, asking questions about their tenure and the way the job was done at that time. Individuals responsible for the training of new members and the ongoing training of existing personnel are also essential sources of information. Who designs the training program, or the training policies? How is training executed? Does a centralized program policy direct the training process, or do less formal rules provide guidance? What are the attitudes toward training? Is it viewed as an essential element of professional participation in the public program, or as a hurdle to be gotten over before the job can get done?

Clearly, a manager must wade through a sea of questions in her or his search of cultural commitments. The questions listed in Box 5.1 can be particularly useful to the manager who is engaged in "soaking and poking" in search of program commitments.

Gathering data through listening and learning will gradually begin to reveal basic continuities, or commitments that define the way work is done in the organization. Managers may take note of the prominence of one profession over others. The role of customers and the role of performance and performance measures; the role of leadership, the relevance of hierarchy, and the care or concern directed toward employees; the loyalty of employees and the relationship between headquarters and branches; and the concern or attention to external oversight, other organizations, and so forth all provide valuable insights into a program's commitments. A simple strategy is to make a list of these wide-ranging observations. Do the observations point to similar patterns, or ways of doing things?

Within the Federal Reserve Board, a commitment to "reasonableness" is evident. The manager soaking in and poking around at the Fed would identify language and processes that reveal this commitment in two forms. First, staff members and governors on the Fed board weigh the consequences of every regulatory action they undertake, carefully considering its impact on the banks, on depositors and customers, and on the communities from which banks draw deposits. Second, staff and governors try to remain consistent in their policymaking by adhering to standards of appropriateness determined within the agency, not by those of the current political moment. Both concerns for measured action and consistency are found in the words of an assistant Federal Reserve Board director responsible for supervisory policy.

Box 5.1 Guide for Identifying Program Commitments

- What language is used in the day-to-day functioning of the organization to describe or refer to the work of the agency?
- What language is used to describe or refer to the clientele or customers?
- What language is used to describe the work of other divisions within the organization or offices?
- What language is used to describe or refer to other relevant organizations?
- What language is used to describe political overseers and the relevance of oversight or political support for the work of the agency?
- What language is used to describe the work of the organization in annual reports and other documents? Is that language an accurate portrayal of program efforts in the eyes of employees?
- What language is used to describe the efforts of current and past leaders? What is their relevance to employees?
- What language is used to describe organizational improvements and failures?
- What stories are told and what kind of examples given?
- How do people behave in an emergency or problem situation? Who has authority or exercises influence in such circumstances? How is the problem resolved?
- What is the design and style of the organization, and where or how are various divisions or offices located?
- What type of education have line and staff employees and members of management received prior to working in the agency?
- How is the training program for newcomers and continuing education opportunities for current employees structured? Where do these programs take place?
- What are the backgrounds of leaders past and present? What courses have their career paths taken since leaving the agency?
- What is the formal design of organizational authority and responsibility and the language used to describe the real power and responsibilities within the agency?
- Is authority centralized or decentralized?

If you took a broad historical view . . . the Fed has been very steady on the course. . . . We have not been hog wild, but we have not been sloughing off either. . . . Others are more responsive to the political winds. . . . There will be some sloughing off, and then [the other agencies] will get religion. . . . When they have fallen off, we get questioned about why we are more demanding, and when they are more intense, we get asked why we are sloughing off. . . . We tend to have the best program . . . [but] consistency is difficult.[17]

These twin concerns for measured caution and consistency, expressed throughout the Fed and evident in its regulatory efforts, can be characterized as a commitment to reasonableness. Another observer might give the commitment an alternative name, or view measured caution and consistency as two distinct but reinforcing program commitments. The labels are not important. What is important is developing a picture of the commitments that drive the way work is done in the Fed. While the FDIC and the OCC also strive to be consistent and to act with caution, in both cases a stronger, more dominant commitment overrides reasonableness as a defining dimension of work in those agencies. The FDIC's commitment to protect the fund and the OCC's commitment to innovation override the influence of "reasonableness" (as pursued by the Fed) as an organizational commitment.

CONNECTING ROOTS TO COMMITMENTS

The final step a manager must undertake to detect cultural commitments is to look for connections between the initial map of the organization's environment, task, and resources and the list of observations about the way that the job gets done. The ESLARP program serves as a good example of this last step. In the early days of ESLARP, when the program was called UEMAP, a "soaking and poking" might have revealed the following list of commitments:

• Expertise is developed within a university setting.
• The researcher is best equipped to determine project selection.
• Regular contact with the residents of East St. Louis is unnecessary to develop and execute a project.

The source of these commitments could readily be connected to the environment, task, and personnel of the project. The relatively autonomous university setting allowed faculty, in their capacity as professional researchers, to define the parameters of a somewhat vague program mandate and to develop the commitments to guide the work of UEMAP. Central to this professional dimension was objectivity, or maintenance of an unbiased distance between the academic planner or designer and the focus of analysis. This fostered an emphasis on individual research projects and designs rather than on support for a working relationship between UEMAP and city residents. The demands of a politician in the state legislature (committee chair of educational appropriations) that faculty focus on the needs of East St. Louis required that a project be established quickly. Start-up of the project was more readily accomplished by giving individual departments and researchers money to conduct projects rather than by developing a collaborative, time-intensive venture.

Identifying the roots of a program, the established commitments, and the connections between the two need not be three separate processes. The connections are sometimes quite obvious and interrelated, as in the case of ESLARP. Professor Reardon began his tenure with a clear picture of the connections between a commitment to academic expertise and the central place of the University of Illinois in the program environment. As a scholar whose work emphasized participatory research, Reardon could also see the ways in which traditional research approaches constrained the building of community partnerships with academicians.

In other instances, making the connections between cultural roots and program commitments can be more complex. The Fed's commitment to reasonableness, for example, evolves not only from the professional influence of personnel trained and with experience in central banking and economics, but also from a carefully constructed interpretation of its mission and the effort to strike a careful balance in a potentially volatile environment. After decades of controversy over whether there was a need for a central bank, and if so what its role ought to be in the economy, Fed leaders gradually focused the bank's efforts on stabilizing the economy through monetary policy determined by the Fed itself.[18] Stabilization requires consideration of a broad range of economic interests, but it also requires taking what might be unpopular steps in order to slow down or speed up the economy. A commitment to reasonableness arises in this context. Fed decisions must be measured for the sake of overall economic health As such it is essential that the Fed maintain a relatively high level of autonomy from elected officials bent on defending economic interests that might be harmed by Fed policy.

A leader of the Fed seeking to change or alter the commitment to reasonableness, or any leader of a public program seeking to make changes in his or her organization, needs to understand the intricate connections between environment, task, and resources on one hand and program commitments on the other. The connections provide a focus for the manager's inward and outward management efforts. The connections can help a manager to see what dimensions of the environment need targeting, what dimensions of the task need changing, and what resources need altering to bring about new commitments.

CONCLUSION

There is no doubt. The culture of a public program can be murky and difficult to detect. Cultural commitments are not necessarily etched in a rulebook, annual report, or mission statement. But commitments are very real dimensions of a public program and its capacity to perform—every bit as real as divisions of authority, office walls, and systems for personnel and budgeting. Mapping the roots of a program culture, and identifying and connecting program commitments to those roots, provides managers with an essential focus for change by helping them identify what needs to change and how that change might be facilitated. The process of detecting cultural commitments requires the ability to listen and the capacity to learn and apply what is learned. The same skills are essential for bringing about change. In Chapter 6 we will take a final look at the successful leadership styles of James Lee Witt, Nicholas Pastore, and Kenneth Reardon. Armed with an understanding of their existing program cultures, each was able to tackle the process of culture change in a manner that other public managers seeking to change their own program cultures will find useful.

Notes

1. Richard Fenno Jr., *Home Style: House Members in Their Districts* (Glenview, Ill.: Scott, Foresman, 1978).

2. Ibid., 249. See also Danny Jorgenson, *Participant Observation* (Thousand Oaks, Calif.: Sage, 1989); and David Fetterman, *Ethnography: Step by Step* (Thousand Oaks, Calif.: Sage, 1998).

3. James Lee Witt, telephone interview with the author, October 24, 2001.

4. A large literature in political science argues that mandates and expectations provide more than a guide to bureaucratic behavior. Congress, it argues, *controls* public organizations. For examples of some of the earliest work in this area, see Morris Fiorina, "Legislative Choice of Regulatory Forms: Legal Process or Administrative Process," *Public Choice* 39 (September 1982): 33–66; and Barry Weingast and Mark Moran, "Bureaucratic Discretion or Congresional Control? Regulatory Policymaking by the Federal Trade Commission," *Journal of Political Economy* 91 (1983): 765–800. For a broader perspective of the attentiveness of public organizations to legislative overseers, see Martha Derthick, *Agency Under Stress: The Social Security Administration in American Government* (Washington, D.C.: Brookings, 1990); and Joel Aberbach, *Keeping a Watchful Eye: The Politics of Congressional Oversight* (Washington, D.C.: Brookings, 1990).

5. Kenneth Reardon, "Institutionalizing Community Service Learning at a Major Research University: The Case of the East St. Louis Action Research Project," *Michigan Journal of Community Service Learning* 4 (1997): 130–136.

6. Kenneth Reardon, telephone interview with author, November 3, 2000.

7. Anne Khademian, *Checking on Banks: Autonomy and Accountability in Three Federal Agencies* (Washington, D.C.: Brookings, 1996).

8. Kenneth Reardon, "Institutionalizing Community Service Learning," 135; and Reardon, interview.

9. For a discussion of the challenges of a customer approach to managing public programs, see Donald Kettl, "Building Lasting Reform: Enduring Questions, Missing Answers," in *Inside the Reinvention Machine: Appraising Governmental Reform*, ed. D. Kettl and J. DiIulio (Washington, D.C.: Brookings, 1995).

10. Eric Yoder, "Mint Condition," Government Exec.com, September 1, 1998. Retrieved from the Web on March 22, 2001, at http://www.govexec.com/features/0998/0998s5.htm.

11. Khademian, *Checking on Banks.*

12. For an interesting comparison of two contrasting views of citizenship (the citizen-as-customer view and the citizen-as-owner view) and their implications for public management, see Hindy Lauer Schachter, "Reinventing Government or Reinventing Ourselves: Two Models for Improving Government Performance," *Public Administration Review* 55 (1995): 530–537. George Frederickson argues that citizens are not customers of government, but owners. See Frederickson, "Painting Bull's Eyes Around Bullet Holes," *Governing*, October 1992, 13.

13. See, for example, the Government Performance and Results Act (GPRA), passed in 1993, which mandates a performance-based budget process. The law required federal agencies to submit the first mandated strategic plans to Congress and the OMB in September 1997. Performance plans were submitted in Spring 1998 that specified performance targets for 1999 and the ways in which day-to-day agency efforts would achieve long-term strategic goals. Annual updates are to be reported. The process is intended to be iterative, whereby the work of each successive stage facilitates the work of agencies, their stakeholders, and elected officials in identifying and eventually utilizing performance data for managing programs and making budget allocations.

14. The National Performance Review, established in 1993 under the leadership of Vice President Al Gore, published numerous reports highlighting the importance of performance and results for government reform and supported legislation converting executive branch agencies to performance-based organizations that would operate under very different rules and expectations. See, for example, National Performance Review, *Performance-Based Organizations: A Conversion Guide* (Washington, D.C.: Government Printing Office, 1997).

15. The Federal Aviation Administration, for example, altered the way its logistics center receives funding in 2000 to emphasize the importance of performance for better customer service. The center's annual appropriation is now given to FAA field offices (primary customer groups for the logistics center) so line managers can determine how much money they will spend on logistics. The center will then have to compete to earn business. See Brian Friel, "Daily Briefing: FAA Logistics Center Cooks Up Reinvention Recipes," Govexec.com, May 27, 1998. Retrieved from the Web on January 11, 1999, at http://www.govexec.com/dailyfed.

16. See Martha Feldman and Anne Khademian, "Principles for Public Management Practice: From Dichotomies to Interdependence," *Governance: An International Journal of Policy and Administration* 14, no. 3 (2001): 339–361, for a discussion of the importance of process in public management.

17. Cited in Khademian, *Checking on Banks*, 136–137.

18. Ibid., 97–99.

Getting the Job Done
with Culture

Lessons Learned and Questions Unanswered

IN THIS BOOK WE MAKE THE CASE for two basic arguments. First, to understand the culture of a public program, we must understand the roots of that culture. Second, to manage the culture of a public program, we must manage the way the roots of a culture weave together. These arguments are drawn from our effort to consolidate collective thinking about the *manageability* of culture and to present that consolidated knowledge as the cultural roots model (Chapter 3). In the text we tested the potential of this model by drawing upon examples of public sector managers who successfully changed culture by getting underneath the surface of a program and focusing their attention upon the roots of culture. In this chapter we will begin by summarizing what we have learned about managing culture and end by pointing out some of the questions we have left unanswered.

LESSONS LEARNED

The primary lesson of advocates of manageability is that leadership makes an enormous difference in the way the job gets done in an organization. Managing culture, the advocates conclude, is the most important responsibility of a leader. The primary lesson of skeptics of manageability is that the environment is an enormous factor in determining the culture of an organization—so big, in fact, that it can and often will overwhelm the efforts of a leader to change or even influence culture. Political pressure, public perceptions, systems of meaning, and in some cases rapid and unpredictable change can dominate the culture that evolves.

The primary lesson of this book is that *both* the advocates and the skeptics are right. Leadership can matter a great deal in developing a culture when leaders are focused not only inward toward the definition of the task and the application of resources and personnel, but outward toward the environment as well. Leaders who change culture in public programs change the way the roots of culture—the task, resources, and environment—weave together. The leaders presented in Chapter 3 each worked to change the environments of the public programs for which they were responsible and alter the understanding of the organization's task and its application of resources to change the commitments driving the way the work was done. What stands out about these three leaders is the way they engaged and managed the integration of the environment, task, and resources. Their leadership styles provide a powerful example for the public manager trying to bring about culture change in his or her organization.

Leadership Style and Culture Change

Kenneth Reardon, James Lee Witt, and Nicholas Pastore held distinct commitments they wanted to foster to bring about change in their respective programs. But each manager engaged, uprooted, and reworked the roots of their program cultures in very similar ways. Each emphasized the importance of listening and learning as leaders. Each broadened the base of participation in their respective public program. Each sought to provide the necessary resources for participants to reach their full potential. Each practiced continuous evaluation of the changes they sought to make. Each targeted authority structures and relationships within their program and outside. And each was relentless in his efforts to rework the roots of culture in his public program (see Box 6.1). Reardon, Witt, and Pastore, in other words, gave careful study to the existing culture and attended to building the capacity of their program to change and develop new commitments.

Listen and Learn. The leaders studied in Chapter 3 were not only careful listeners, but were also able to apply what they had learned. They continuously listened to employees, partners, members of the public, politicians, and other program managers to learn the way participants understood the basic tasks of their programs, the way resources and skills were applied to approach these tasks, and the dynamics of the environment surrounding the programs. And each leader learned from the information they gathered, effectively applying those lessons to their efforts to manage the roots of culture.

Reardon began his tenure with ESLARP by driving three hours to the city of East St. Louis to ask the residents how a partnership with the university could work. He used the information and concerns of residents to begin to build an interdisciplinary collaboration with neighborhood organizations and residents. By listening to the residents and building their concerns into the program structure, Reardon established the trust that was essential for a partnership to grow based upon shared responsibility for the work of ESLARP.

Witt began his term with FEMA by standing in front of the elevators to listen and talk to his employees, meeting with any employee who wanted to talk every Tuesday morning, and walking around the agency and flying around the country

Box 6.1 Dimensions of Leadership That Facilitate Culture Change

- Listen and learn from the information gathered.
- Look for ways to broaden the base of participation.
- Identify and provide resources to enable all participants to excel.
- Practice continuous evaluation.
- Target authority structures within and without the program.
- Be relentless.

listening to partners in emergency management and to the victims of disasters. Utilization of this daily information, along with that gleaned from surveys of victims of natural disasters and from the experiences of partners and employees, drove the effort to revamp FEMA.

As chief of police in New Haven, Connecticut, Pastore built a community-based policing program by listening to people in the community. He met, listened to, and learned from residents of the community while walking the beat with his officers, attending neighborhood gatherings, playing gin rummy in the park, and holding special seminars and classes that brought police officers together with different populations within New Haven. Pastore listened to the officers on the beat, and he listened to their supervisors. He listened to organizations in the private sector seeking to develop partnerships with the police like the CD–CP mental health partnership with physicians and other mental health clinicians in the Yale Child Study Center. And he learned from all of that listening, working to build sensitivity training, mediation skills, and competencies in complex issues such as the mental health needs and treatment of children into the training and everyday work of the police force.

In Chapter 5 we saw how listening and learning, or "soaking and poking," to use Richard Fenno's phrase, allows us to unearth the roots of a program culture and identify the commitments that drive the way the job gets done, and permits us to make the connections between the two. These observations aid us in creating a map of an existing program culture. And knowing what exists allows us to focus management efforts where they are most needed to successfully effect culture change.

Encourage Participation. Each of the three leaders in Chapter 3 encouraged broad participation in the development and implementation of their respective programs.[1] By broadening the base of participation to include more employees, outside organizations, and members of the public, Reardon, Witt, and Pastore not only were able to identify the established ways of getting the work done but also were able to expand on that information and adopt newly available ideas about how to get things done that allowed participants to think differently about the programs. Creating more opportunities for participation also helped build loyalty among participants who became as committed to change as their respective managers.

Witt turned over the agenda for reforming FEMA to senior managers gathered at a retreat and gave every employee the opportunity to contribute ideas for improvement. He created opportunities for private businesses to partner with FEMA in disaster relief and broadened the educational mission of FEMA in disaster prevention to engage communities across the country in the effort. As a former emergency management director from the state of Arkansas, Witt understood the need for making state emergency management personnel, as well as a wide range of organizations involved in disaster relief, regular partners in the work of FEMA. This expansion of participation to include businesses, nonprofit organizations, members of the public, and emergency management personnel across the country helped to turn critics in FEMA's environment into committed partners, and to build the capacity of FEMA to implement its newly articulated mission emphasizing relief, mitigation, and prevention. For Witt, increased participation, particularly on the part of FEMA employees, was essential for a better-performing agency. In Witt's own words,

> It doesn't hurt us to say thank you to someone. It doesn't hurt us to share information with the people that we're managing. Because someone may have an idea that may not be a big idea, but someone else may have another idea, and both of them together could create a fantastic program. Or a fantastic change. To make it better to serve our customers or each other.[2]

Reardon built ESLARP on the concept of participatory research spreading the base of participation to include city residents and organizations, university students, and faculty from across the university. If Reardon was to build a partnership, residents needed to be included not only in the discussion of problems and potential solutions, but in the research, design and implementation of projects intended to address the city's problems. Inclusion of the residents was essential to uprooting the approach to urban renewal based upon a hierarchy of expertise and to loosening the hold on authority of the academic community over the identification, research, and development of solutions to urban problems. Inclusion of University of Illinois undergraduate and graduate students provided essential labor to conduct massive research efforts, help organize residents and organizations for tackling the political environment, and build a cadre of future professional planners and architects skilled in the practice of participatory research.

Pastore expanded police and community participation through the creation of programs like the CD–CP mental health partnership. Police officers were given the opportunity and responsibility for contributing to the treatment of children exposed to violence. Through fellowships with the police, weekly case conferences, and responding to police officers who paged them, mental health clinicians became part of a community approach to addressing the needs of children. And community-based organizations also became part of the effort to address the needs of each individual child. For Pastore, a community-based approach to policing meant making the neighborhoods and neighborhood organizations part of the policing effort—and ultimately expanding the definition of what it meant to police a community.

Each leader viewed a broad base of participation as a means to facilitate change in the environment, in the application of resources, and in the perception of the task and as a means to build support for change.

Provide Resources for Participants to Advance. The leaders in Chapter 3 understood as one of their primary responsibilities the provision of resources to advance the knowledge and skills of their employees, and in some cases participants outside of the immediate program. To change the way people understand the task at hand, and the way resources and skills are applied to that task, participants need new capacities—that is, increased knowledge and improved skills. Even beyond the initial changes in program cultures, the three leaders viewed opportunities for educational advancement and growth among program participants as essential ingredients for maintaining a healthy public program with the ability to evolve with the public's needs.[3]

Under the leadership of Pastore, police officers in New Haven, Connecticut, were trained in the techniques of community policing, with an emphasis upon their role in addressing the needs of children exposed to violence. Senior officers attended mental health seminars at Yale University that focused on the needs of children exposed to violence. Weekly case reviews between police officers and mental health clinicians provided the officers steady exposure to the expertise of mental health professionals and mental health clinicians a better understanding of their own role in addressing the needs of children. This ongoing training helped each profession to see how it could blend and work in partnership with the other, facilitating a core commitment of the CD–CP mental health partnership. Pastore viewed the professional growth of officers, in particular, as a key component of his leadership responsibilities. He sought to provide his officers with the necessary resources to exercise their discretion as participants in the mental health partnership. In Pastore's words, "You have to have a philosophy in place. As a leader, your chief job is to create a support net of resources to facilitate . . . their thinking." [4]

One of the most important lessons Reardon learned from listening to residents of East St. Louis was the need to make available to them a range of educational opportunities without which they could not participate as equal partners in ESLARP. If residents lacked the basic theoretical knowledge and academic skills available to faculty and students, then the partnership could not be complete. The Neighborhood College was established to offer courses to any resident of East St. Louis for free, with course options driven by resident priorities and interests. ESLARP's daily implementation of participatory research created educational opportunities for residents to learn planning and research skills, and educated students and faculty about the challenges of life in the inner city and provided new skills and ideas for approaching urban renewal.

With Witt at the helm, each employee of FEMA was required to undertake training in customer service. The commitment to customer service was also fostered by Witt's encouragement of all employees to think outside the box, or to approach problems in creative ways and to find solutions built around the best interests of FEMA's customers. Witt viewed his employees as essential customers, too, and encouraged them to find ways to advance their individual skills to be better problem solvers and happier individuals. Beyond FEMA employees, Witt reached out to individual communities and businesses to educate them about disaster relief, mitigation, and preparation—in essence, training them to think differently about their own responsibilities in the event of a disaster and reconsider how they might better contribute to FEMA's mandated efforts.

For the managers of ESLARP, FEMA, and the CD–CP mental health partnership, more knowledgeable and better-trained participants were essential to the development of more responsive and effective organizations.[5]

Evaluate and Think Critically about Changes.   Evaluation of the changes in each program was also an essential component of the leadership styles of Ken Reardon, Nick Pastore, and James Lee Witt. Managing the roots of a program culture requires continuous effort. Environments metamorphose, resources fluctuate, personnel come and go, and the task can be changed by a new mandate or a new partnership. The leaders in Chapter 3 pursued continuous evaluation of the way environment, task, and resources came together to keep their respective programs focused on the commitments they sought to establish as the driving forces of ESLARP, FEMA, and the CD–CP mental health partnership.

ESLARP's annual retreats opened up every dimension of the program for scrutiny and discussion. Continuous evaluation advanced the program from one built on participatory research to one that included direct action organizing to one that embraced community education through the Neighborhood College. Weekly meetings between police and mental health professionals in the CD–CP partnership provided opportunities not only to think critically and broadly about individual cases, but also to think differently about the ways in which the program was working. And continuous feedback from victims of disaster, partners at the state and local levels, and FEMA employees themselves aided FEMA to better focus on its mission of relief, mitigation, and disaster prevention. In addition, reward systems were built into the agency to encourage the kind of critical thinking that advanced the efforts of FEMA.

Challenge Established Authority Relations. The leaders in Chapter 3 worked to alter established authority relations both within and outside of their respective programs. Cultural commitments are held in place by practice and the understanding participants have of where power and authority rest. To change the integration of the roots of culture requires the shaking up of traditional understandings of authority—where it is located, who has it, and how it can be used. This includes the sharing with employees and other participants in a public program of authority vested in the leader.[6]

Witt broke up the directorates of FEMA and created new departments centered on FEMA's mission. Information once held tightly within former directorates as a source of authority became widely communicated and shared throughout FEMA and with FEMA partners. To improve FEMA's capacity to provide relief, mitigation, and disaster prevention, more participants needed more information, and more people within FEMA needed permission to exercise their individual authority to make decisions and serve customers. Pastore broke down traditional perceptions of police authority based upon intervention after the fact, or after a crime was committed. As partners in the CD–CP mental health partnership officers were empowered to work with children, neighborhoods, and community organizations to address the needs of children exposed to violence and to find ways to prevent violence in the first place. And Reardon's approach to participatory research challenged conventional planning practices as well as academic approaches to research and the criteria for rewarding the work of faculty. Reardon worked to establish community engagement as an essential dimension of the university mission, and to make residents a permanent component of urban planning and renewal. In Reardon's words,

> Universities need projects like ESLARP to renew themselves. . . . This was the [great hope of the early university movement] . . . to bring faculty out of the ivory towers. . . . It was the American idea of the new American college . . . bringing benefits to the community and young people learning of democracy and undemocracy. . . . Rediscovering the soul and the special role of the university in the commons.[7]

Each leader, in short, worked to uproot an existing culture in part by challenging the authority built into the traditional way of getting the job done.

Be Relentless. Finally, in their efforts to manage the roots of culture, the leaders studied in Chapter 3 had to be relentless in pursuing the changes they sought to make. In order to facilitate open communication and a commitment to customer service, Witt had to practice both every day. He did this by walking around, listening, and learning from a variety of sources and by sharing information with members of Congress and numerous other FEMA partners in an ongoing effort to improve communication. And Witt not only continuously sought ways to focus employees on serving the customer, but also treated employees as valued customers of the agency eligible for advancement and rewards in recognition of their hard work and good ideas.

Despite intense criticism, Pastore throughout his tenure relentlessly sought to better understand the community that he served and to create community partnerships with other professionals such as mental health clinicians. His support for a needle exchange program to reduce the transfer of disease through intravenous drug use, the demotion of senior members of the department to parole officer status, and his appointment as a white chief of police by New Haven's first African American mayor all stood as obstacles to his efforts. But he was relentless in supporting a training program based upon understanding New Haven's neighborhood residents, empowering officers to play a role in preventing violence and treating its aftermath, and engaging the community in supporting his efforts.

Finally, shared responsibility and continuous evaluation guided the daily efforts of Ken Reardon as well. For Reardon, each day was an opportunity to find ways to improve the effectiveness of a university–resident partnership, to build the support of the university for this collaboration, and to find ways to do the work of ESLARP better—ways identified by residents, students, faculty, and any other ESLARP partner willing to contribute to the program's improvement.

Focus Leadership Style on Building the Capacity to Change. Despite very different public programs, different personnel and resources, and different locations, the leaders of the New Haven Police Department, ESLARP and FEMA practiced the changes they sought to bring about through a similar style of leadership. Their ability to listen, learn, and evaluate, and their efforts to broaden participation, help employees develop the skills to participate, and alter the original distributions of authority in the program, were all essential for uprooting existing cultures and reweaving the roots of culture into new program commitments.

Simply put, the manner in which each of these managers led their programs was key to the change in their program's culture. They concerned themselves with understanding the existing commitments and focused on the processes needed to facilitate change. *How* culture would change was as important as the end itself— a change in culture. Yet in a world where politicians, the public, and managers emphasize and celebrate results and seek ways to get results in a more efficient manner, this message is a difficult one to grasp. A thoughtful analysis of community policing as a concept and guide for the work of police departments warns against efforts that elevate the means of community policing over the ultimate ends.[8] Community policing efforts focused on a broad attempt to engage the community can become "just an effort to reduce tensions between the police and the community and to generate more positive community attitudes toward the police."[9] The number of meetings with the community and the number of participants attending those meetings can quickly become measures of police success, while "the effect on robbery," for example, can be less clear.[10] The means of conducting community policing and accommodating broad participation from the community can quickly overcome the ultimate ends of community policing—that is, reducing crime.

This caution is critical, particularly as participation in public programs becomes broader through partnerships with a variety of public, private, and nonprofit organizations and the public at large.[11] Managers must not lose sight of the targeted goals for the public programs they direct even as they create opportunities for participation on a broad scale. But the caution nevertheless represents a tendency, accelerated by results-oriented reforms, to neglect the details of *how* results ought to come about—indeed, how results ought to be identified in the first place. An evaluation of the National Performance Review, launched by Vice President Al Gore in 1993, observed, "Stripped of the rhetoric and stories, improving government performance is fundamentally about people and the tools they need to do their jobs."[12] Whether or not participants in a public program move toward expectations for performance depends upon the availability and application of essential tools and skills to pursue a task, and the capacity of individuals and organizations that can develop in the course of pursuing that task. A manager focused on how individual and organizational capacity is built not only helps to build the essential infrastructure to carry out public programs into the future, but might learn of better, alternative ways of accomplishing program expectations and even worthy expectations not previously articulated. In the case of community policing, a chief of police must focus on how the police force engages the community and the evolving capacity to conduct policing in the form of a partnership with the community. Placing attention on these vital issues of process will help to foster trust, which is essential if community policing is to take hold and be an effective means to reduce crime. This process of trust building was an essential component of the CD–CP mental health partnership that today serves to prevent and reduce violence in New Haven.

The connection between the *means* of managing culture and the *end* (a changed culture and better performance) is intimately connected to how a leader approaches the task of culture change and helps define the culture that emerges. The daily effort to change the way the program interacts with its environment, the way participants understand and approach the task at hand, and the skills and resources people bring to the task are inseparable from the culture change itself. Just as a police officer must learn to engage members of the neighborhood beat to develop a professional yet comfortable rapport, the officer must practice engagement to make it an effective tool for community policing. As individual leaders, Nicholas Pastore, James Lee Witt, and Kenneth Reardon practiced the changes they sought, but they also used their clout as leaders to provide resources and facilitate the capacity of individuals and organizations to practice those changes. This approach stands as a solid example of effective leadership, valuable to any public manager contemplating change.

Sustaining Culture

The leaders of ESLARP, FEMA, and the CD–CP mental health partnership sought to change their program cultures. Not every manager wants to bring about such dramatic change, however. Sometimes the challenge is simply maintenance of a culture viewed to be productive and useful. A lesson drawn from other examples in the text is that the task of sustaining a culture is similar to the task of change. To sustain a culture requires an understanding of the commitments driving the program, the connection of commitments to cultural roots, and an ongoing effort to engage the roots to maintain the preferred commitments.

Sustaining the culture of the Federal Reserve, for example, has required the careful attention of leaders to the integration of environment, resources, and skills, and the understanding of the task facing the agency. Over the Fed's long history, a commitment to reasonableness in its supervision of banks has emerged. The commitment is embedded in the agency's broader task of managing the nation's supply of money. A reasonable approach to supervision reflects, first, a potentially volatile environment of diverse economic interests and elected officials anxious to support constituent interests. To lean toward one interest or segment of the economy too heavily would be to agitate economic interests and their political representatives, and could challenge longstanding procedures for conducting oversight and insuring the accountability of the nation's central bank. Those procedures of accountability are built upon Fed leaders routinely reporting before Congress on the economy and Fed policy, but presenting that information in a very cautious manner supported by extensive research conducted by Fed economists and other staff. Second, a commitment to reasonableness represents the influence of senior staff members who are somewhat insulated from political pressure and thereby able to impose measured judgment and experience on policy and rules. The Fed's autonomy also allows the expertise of economists, supervisors, and other staff skilled in banking to flourish and hence helps to shape a reasonable approach to policymaking. Finally, a commitment to reasonableness represents an understanding of the Fed's primary task as "leaning against the wind"—slowing the economy through monetary policy when it speeds up and giving it a boost when it slows down. This and other commitments would not be sustained if Fed leaders did not continuously attend to the fluctuating economic and political environment, maintain the Fed approach to the task at hand, and provide support for the professional work of economists and other staff members.

In contrast, the culture of the South African Police Service (SAPS) has lingered without an alternative, in large part because of the inability of its recent leaders to uproot and manage established commitments. Whether due to the tenacity of SAPS program roots or to the inability of recent leaders to find ways to engage that culture and promote change, the existing culture will linger and drift until the roots of the culture weave together in a different way. The current leader of Safety and Security, Stephen Vukile Tshwete, has begun to disturb program culture by engaging the roots. Most critically, he has begun to focus on the basic definition and understanding of the task facing police and has begun to apply resources to support rigorous enforcement of the law rather than policing civil unrest. His biggest challenge will be the environment of SAPS. Fledgling communities that do not trust the police, politicians who want crime controlled but are fearful of a powerful police force, and an international environment teeming with consultants and researchers anxious to advise the police on how best to achieve reform create distinct expectations and pressures for police performance. Tshwete might tackle the task by listening to and learning from employees and diverse voices in the environment and by focusing on building the capacity of individual officers and the organization to change by sharing resources and communicating information. Or he might try to tighten the controls he has over resources, limit participation, limit communication, and try to navigate the environment by shutting it out. The latter is a common response for programs under siege.[13] The first approach, while not an instinctive response, could nevertheless be a necessary response to begin to uproot and reroot the SAPS culture.

Whether changing or sustaining a culture, a leader is only one part of the equation. Leaders must identify the roots of a culture and the commitments that define the culture, and they must be able to understand the connection between the two. They must then work to engage the roots to change and even maintain a culture embedded in potentially volatile environments, routine applications of personnel and resources, and often a long-established understanding of the task.

Thinking Broadly and Creatively about the Program Environment

Finally, the examples in this book should encourage managers seeking to change culture to think broadly and creatively about the environments of their programs. For a public program, the formal political environment is most prominent. The city council, state legislature, or Congress; the mayor's office, governor's office, or White House; interest groups; judicial decisions regarding program implementation; and any personnel, budget, or policy guidelines specified in the mandate or by executive order all have a prominent place in the program environment. But beyond elected officials, formal rules, structures, and processes are norms, values, and customs; systems of meaning; informal relations with organizations and constituencies; and public perceptions. Judgments about a program's contribution, its value as a source of expertise, and its responsiveness to its clientele, for example, rest on less formal parameters, but these parameters are nevertheless important for the implementation of a program. Public policies targeting different groups of people, such as children, elderly people, prisoners, or middle-class families, reflect social judgments about the value of the target population, its dependency, levels of deviance, or privileged status within society.[14] Not only do these judgments have consequences for the targeted populations, but they also have consequences for how political overseers communicate with an agency responsible for the program, check its actions, and intervene on behalf of constituencies.

Reardon, Pastore, and Witt each held an expansive view of their respective program environments and used that perspective for engaging the environment as a root of program culture. Reardon understood public perceptions of poverty in the inner city and had a broad perspective of economic and political factors that pushed East St. Louis to severe decline. He used that information to expose negative stereotypes and to frame educational experiences for all ESLARP participants. Creating a more realistic understanding of life in East St. Louis fostered a common ground among participants—one based upon mutual respect—and hence facilitated the commitment to shared responsibility. Without a broader perspective of the ESLARP environment, however, significant differences in perception might have impeded the work of the program.

James Lee Witt faced an angry environment when he took office: Members of Congress were extremely critical of the agency's performance, governors and mayors and state-level emergency management personnel were dismayed, and victims of disaster were distraught by their encounters with FEMA. But in his analysis of FEMA's environment, Witt went deeper. He saw the different perceptions, or systems of meaning, that influenced disaster relief at the state and local level relative to those influencing relief efforts at the national level. The emphasis on protecting the government after a nuclear attack—and hence secrecy—drove much of FEMA's pre-1990s work. Different directorates in the agency had connections to the Department of Defense, where these systems of meaning were fostered. In contrast, disaster relief at the state and local levels was focused on the immediate needs of victims and communities in disasters. Understanding these two distinct perceptions, each framed by different experiences, helped Witt to revamp FEMA to play a facilitating role for state and local emergency relief efforts across the board.

Nicholas Pastore was a student of police history. He ground his efforts to revitalize the New Haven Police Department and to build the CD–CP mental health partnership in his understanding of the system of meaning that had framed police work for more than a hundred years—to protect the status quo. When Pastore looked to the city of New Haven, he saw not only people to be served, but people with very different experiences and needs and hence with very different relationships to the police. Perceiving and understanding these environmental differences was built into officer training and the work of programs like the CD–CP mental health partnership.

Even in programs as stable as the FDIC, understanding subtle yet critical aspects of the environment is essential for maintaining program culture. Public confidence in the banking system is built in part around the security of a bank insurance fund. Understanding the dimensions of public confidence is critical not only for guiding FDIC policy, but also for finding ways to maintain protection of the fund as a central commitment of the agency's culture.

While the environmental factors influencing a public program can be subtle, they are nevertheless important to the development of a culture. Public managers need to look beyond the immediate political environment to understand the multitude of influences that can affect program culture. They need to be able to think carefully about how to engage, expose, or utilize those influences to facilitate change.

UNANSWERED QUESTIONS

In this book we have focused on public programs. However, it is pertinent to ask whether the cultural roots model is relevant or applicable for organizations in the private sector as well. Are there significant differences in the environment and in leadership flexibility between the private and public sectors, and if so, do these differences affect the formation and change of culture?

The Environment and Public and Private Cultures

A primary difference between cultures in the public and private sectors could be the overwhelming relevance to the former of the environment. This is not to say that the environment is not a factor for private organizations. Both public and private organizations face uncertainty and must navigate a diverse set of stakeholders in pursuit of their goals.[15] And a corporation out of touch with its environment would not be in business for very long. But perhaps the difference rests with the *ways* in which the environment matters to public programs versus private organizations. In matters of degree, public programs might experience the environment more as a set of constraints, expectations, and pressures, while the private organization might experience the environment less as a constraint and more as an opportunity. Public programs operate under the aegis of elected officials, interest groups, myriad mandates, and overlapping jurisdictions. While public managers certainly can find opportunity in these environments, and find ways to alter or ease these constraints, the degree of opportunity could be much less than that presented to the private sector leader. What we don't know is whether the environment, as a root of culture, plays a more significant role in a public-sector program than it does in a private-sector organization, and, if it does, why?

Leadership and Public and Private Cultures

Does the degree of control a leader has over the definition of the task matter for the way in which task, resources, and the environment are integrated? A private-sector leader is constrained by the basic capacity of an organization, the board of directors, members of the public as consumers, and shareholders in bringing clarity or redefinition to the task at hand. A public-sector manager, however, is constrained by a mandate or mandates, legislative committees, elected executives, civil service and procurement systems, interest groups, and public perceptions of the program. A private-sector manager might have the flexibility to redefine or reemphasize the task of an organization, as long as the effort produces profits. In the public sector, however, clear bottom lines by which to judge performance are hard to come by as everyone's concept of what constitutes public program performance can differ greatly.

How significant are these differences for the evolution of a culture, and do differences in degree give a private-sector leader more influence over the integration of task, resources, and environment than it gives to a public manager?

CONCLUSION

Culture advocates have demonstrated the importance of a leader in taking the initiative for culture change. Over the past decade scholars, reformers, and practicing public managers have demonstrated the great potential of a public manager to bring about, in some cases, phenomenal change in the way public programs perform. Yet in our enthusiasm for public-management leadership that is entrepreneurial and progressive we must not forget to heed the vast body of research and experience demonstrating that there are particular constraints and limitations under which public managers must operate. Unlike the proverbial "red tape," which is always a target for eradication, the constraints upon public managers are essential products of a democratic system of governance that spreads accountability across three branches of government, all of which are accessible in varying degrees to a broad public of individuals and organized groups.

Public managers can bring about change in the way the job gets done in public programs. But to do so requires a view of culture that goes beyond dictating from above the way work should be done. It requires a broad perspective of the ways in which the task is integrated with resources and personnel and complex environmental factors. To change culture requires working with this process of integration, seeking to understand, work with, and change elements of the environment, resources, and personnel and the task at hand. The leadership styles of Pastore, Witt, and Reardon facilitated the process of culture change in their respective programs. They were able to change program commitments by listening, learning, evaluating, and relentlessly practicing the changes they sought and by focusing on the essential components of change such as the capacities of individuals and organizations to try and eventually support alternative ways of getting the job done.

Environments vary across public programs, and the roots of some public programs run more deeply than others. Yet regardless of the depth of roots or the differences in environment, the task of a public manager trying to use culture as a means to change program performance is the same: Learn about and map the roots of culture and identify basic commitments and then connect those commitments to the roots. Managers must then engage and manage the roots of culture to facilitate changing or sustaining commitments needed to get the job done. This is the task facing present and future leaders of SAPS; the task facing leaders of the Fed, FDIC, and SEC; and the task facing present and future leaders of the New Haven Department of Police Services, FEMA, and ESLARP. The leadership styles of Reardon, Pastore, and Witt suggest one way others might tackle the challenge.

Culture can be elusive, and the task of managing the roots of cultures might feel a bit like weaving smoke. But if program managers do not take on the challenge, the roots of culture will find an alternative path of integration—perhaps in a productive and useful manner, perhaps geared toward mere survival. Culture can be elusive, absolutely. But it can also be a means to bring about new approaches to the implementation of public policy where past efforts have wavered or failed.

Notes

1. For a discussion of inclusive management efforts, see Martha Feldman and Anne Khademian, "Managing for Inclusion: Balancing Control and Participation," *International Public Management Journal* 3, no. 2 (2001): 149–167.

2. Remarks of James Lee Witt, "Closing Plenary: Leadership, Communicating our Leadership with the Public," Discovery 2000, National Park Service General Conference, September 11–15, 2000. Retrieved from the Web, January 2001, http://www.nps.gov/discovery2000/leader/plenary-2.htm.

3. More than fifty years ago organizational theorists argued that the key to successful organizations was successful individuals, and that individual success could be nurtured in democratic organizations or organizations that encouraged

broad participation. The more opportunities to participate in the development and implementation of organization work, the greater the opportunity for individuals to realize their full potential. And the greater the opportunities for "self-actualization," the more productive and successful the organization would be. The arguments of the "humanists," as they were called, placed concern for the individual and opportunities for growth on a par with structural design and procedure in determining organizational success. See H. Metcaff and L. Urwick, *Dynamic Administration: The Collected Papers of Mary Parker Follett* (New York: Harper, 1942); Abraham Maslow, "A Theory of Human Motivation," *Psychological Review* 50 (1943): 370–396; and Douglas McGregor, *The Human Side of Enterprise* (New York: McGraw-Hill, 1960). However, see Charles Perrow, *Complex Organizations: A Critical Essay*, 3d ed. (New York: McGraw-Hill, 1986), 79–96, for a critical review of this approach.

4. Nicholas Pastore, telephone interview with author, November 12, 2001.

5. Providing participants with essential knowledge and resources to exercise individual expertise is considered an essential component of an organization able to learn, or flex and grow. See Peter Senge, *The Fifth Discipline: The Art and Practice of the Learning Organization* (New York: Doubleday-Currency, 1990); S. Spear, "The Emergence of Learning Communities," *The Systems Thinker* 4 (1993): 11–14; Edgar Schein, "The Three Cultures of Management: Implications for Organizational Learning," *Sloan Management Review* 38 (1996): 9–20; and Patrick Townsend, *Commit to Quality* (New York: Wiley, 1990).

6. Gary Miller offers an interesting examination of business executives who "shared hierarchy" to build particularly successful organizations. See Miller, *Managerial Dilemmas: The Political Economy of Hierarchy* (Cambridge: Cambridge University Press, 1992).

7. Kenneth Reardon, telephone interview with author, November 3, 2000.

8. Jean-Paul Brodeur, "Tailor-Made Policing: A Conceptual Investigation," in *How To Recognize Good Policing*, ed. J. P. Brodeur (Thousand Oaks, Calif.: Police Executive Research Forum and Sage, 1998), 30–51. Brodeur cites Herman Goldstein's term "the means over ends syndrome." See Goldstein, "Improving Police: A Problem-Oriented Approach," in *Crime and Delinquency* 25 (1979): 236–258.

9. Brodeur, "Tailor-Made Policing," 41.

10. The example of declines in robbery is taken from Goldstein, "Improving Police: A Problem-Oriented Approach."

11. See, for example, Steven Rathgeb Smith and Michael Lipsky, *Nonprofits for Hire: The Welfare State in the Age of Contracting* (Cambridge: Harvard University Press, 1993); and Helen Ingram and Steven Rathgeb Smith, eds., *Public Policy for Democracy* (Washington, D.C.: Brookings, 1993).

12. Donald Kettl, "Building Lasting Reform: Enduring Questions, Missing Answers," in *Inside the Reinvention Machine*, ed. D. Kettl and J. DiIulio (Washington, D.C.: Brookings, 1995), 23.

13. Barbara Romzek and Melvin Dubnick present an analysis of NASA under similar circumstances. See Romzek and Dubnick, "Accountability in the Public Sector: Lessons from the Challenger Tragedy," *Public Administration Review* 47 (1987): 227–238.

14. Helen Ingram and Anne Schneider, "Constructing Citizenship: The Subtle Messages of Policy Design," in *Public Policy For Democracy*, ed. Helen Ingram and Steven Rathgeb Smith (Washington, D.C.: Brookings, 1993).

15. Mark Moore argues that the differences between public and private organizations are minimal. See Moore, *Creating Public Value: Strategic Management in Government* (Cambridge: Harvard University Press, 1995), 63–65.

Index

Aberbach, Joel, 122
Accountability for program, 112–113
Adams, Guy, 29, 40
Adnopoz, Jean, 82, 106
Advisory Council on Executive Reorganization, 36
Advocates for culture as management tool, 17–24, 124, 137
African National Congress (ANC), 97, 98
Andrejasich, Mike, 69
Andrews, John, 37
Armajani, Babak, 13
Arnold, Peri, 36
Artifacts in organizational culture, 19, 20
Ash, Roy, 36
Aucoin, Peter, 41
Autonomy, 32, 34, 59, 92–95, 104, 133

Ban, Carolyn, 39
Bank regulatory agencies, 92–96, 113–115, 118–121. *See also specific agency (e.g., Federal Reserve Board)*
Barnard, Chester, 17, 18, 22, 36, 37
Barzelay, Michael, 13
Basic assumptions in organizational culture, 18, 19
Basic elements of culture, 20
Beck, Nathaniel, 40
Behn, Robert, 40, 83
Bennis, Warren, 37
Berkman, Miriam, 82, 106
Beyer, Janice, 36, 38, 39, 41
"Bootstrap" rule, 56
Brodeur, Jean-Paul, 139
Brownlow, Louis, 36
Brownlow committee, 15, 36
Bryson, John, 14, 87
Business influence on public management, 31

Cable television show to reach community, 64
Capitalizing on and institutionalizing change, 78–80
Career employees, 35, 96
Caro, Robert, 36
Carter, Jimmy, 50
CD–CP. *See* Child Development–Community Policing
Challenging established authority relations, 130
Changes in culture
    autonomy and, 93
    determining and articulating change, 48, 61–65
    environmental factors defeating efforts for, 96
    examples of, 11–12, 42–43
    how to change, 9–10, 43
    incremental changes, 49
    relentless management efforts to accomplish, 49, 75–78, 130–131
    strategies of managing for, 47–49, 105
    successful leadership styles for, 109, 125–133
Child Development–Community Policing (CD–CP). *See also* Pastore, Nicholas
    building capacity to change, 131–132
    cultural change of, 42, 80–82, 91
    determining and articulating cultural change, 64–65
    environment of, 135–136
    evaluations of changes, 91, 129
    external environment, efforts to change, 73
    identification of commitment, 52
    institutionalizing change, 79
    nature of task, 58–59
    relentless practice of changes, 78, 131

141

Child Development–Community Policing (CD–CP) *continued*

    resources and personnel, 60
    shared leadership, 74–75, 130
    training of police, 128
Cohen, Donald, 52, 74
Commitments, 3–5, 108–123
    connections with cultural roots, 47–48, 53–61, 120–121
    determining and articulating new commitments, 48, 61–65
    ESLARP participants, 3–5
    getting clear picture of, 109–117
    identification of, 47, 49–53, 104, 117–120
    inhibiting innovation and client service, 48
    map of program commitments, 109, 121, 126
    as navigation tool, 26
    of participants, 46
    of public managers, 16
    task, manager's understanding of, 110–111
Communication. *See specific project or agency*
Community Outreach Partnership Center (COPC), 56, 76, 84, 87
Community policing. *See* Child Development–Community Policing (CD–CP)
Competitive advantage, 18
Competitors, 113–114
Comptroller of the Currency. *See* Office of the Comptroller of the Currency (OCC)
Cooperative Extension Service (University of Illinois), 114
COPC. *See* Community Outreach Partnership Center
Creative thinking about environment, 134–136
Crosby, Barbara, 14, 87
Cultural artifacts. *See* Artifacts in organizational culture
Cultural changes. *See* Changes in culture
Cultural roots, 9–10, 42–87
    capitalizing on and institutionalizing change, 78–80, 101–103
    connections with commitments, 47–48, 53–61, 120–121
    determining and articulating change, 48, 61–65
    environment as factor in, 54–57
    essence of culture, 88–92, 104
    extending model of, 88–107

    framework, 42–87
    identification of commitments, 47, 49–53, 109–117
    integration of tasks, resources, and environment, 43, 45–48, 53, 125
    internal and external management of culture, 48–49, 65–73
    production of culture, 44–47
    relentless practice of desired changes, 49, 75–78, 130–131
    resources and personnel, role of, 59–61
    shared responsibility as part of managing, 48–49, 65–66, 74–75, 130
    strategies of managing for change, 47–49, 105
    task's nature as factor in, 57–59
Culture. *See also headings starting with "Cultural"*
    as integrating force, 18–22
    as management tool, 5–7, 15–41. *See also* Debate over culture as management tool
    need to understand, 3–5
    production of, 44–47
Customer service approach of FEMA, 72, 91, 129
Customers of public programs, 114–116

Daft, Richard, 38
Deal, Terrence, 13, 37, 38, 39
Debate over culture as management tool, 15–41
    advocates for, 17–24, 124, 137
    commitment as navigation tool, 25–27
    environment's importance, 25–27
    fragmented culture and environments, 27
    importance of leadership, 22–24
    influence by default, 28–30
    influence by design, 30–31
    influence by transplant, 31–33
    as integrating force, 18–22
    skeptics toward, 24–33, 124
    symbols and systems of meaning, 28
Defense, Department of, 32, 135
de Klerk, F. W., 97, 98
Deming, W. Edwards, 40
Departments, governmental. *See specific names (e.g., Defense, Department of)*
Derthick, Martha, 39, 83, 122
DiMaggio, Paul, 40
Disaster handling. *See* Federal Emergency Management Agency (FEMA)

Dodge, Lowell, 84
Drug Policy Foundation, 86, 87
Drunk driving, 30
Dubnick, Melvin, 40, 82, 140

East St. Louis, Ill., 1, 10, 51, 54–55, 113. *See also* East St. Louis Action Research Project (ESLARP)
East St. Louis Action Research Project (ES-LARP). *See also* Reardon, Kenneth
    Note: From 1987–1992, this project was known as the Urban Extension and Minority Access Project (UEMAP).
    accountability of, 112–113
    attitudes of East St. Louis residents toward, 56, 67, 76, 128
    background of, 1–2, 54–55, 110
    belief system of participants, 89
    commitments of participants, 3–5
    connecting roots to commitments, 120–121
    cultural change of, 2–3, 10–12, 42, 55–56, 80–82, 91–92
    customers of, 115
    definition of task, 110–111
    determining and articulating change, 61–62
    environment of, 54–57, 135
    evaluation annually of efforts, 4, 76, 129
    evaluation by community women, 76, 87
    external environment, efforts to manage, 71
    faculty involvement, 68–69, 111
    funding, 55, 71, 111
    institutionalizing change, 79
    internal management of culture, 67–69
    nature of task to revitalize city, 57
    Neighborhood College created. *See* East St. Louis Neighborhood College
    partnership building, 91, 112, 121, 127, 128
    reasons why UEMAP was failing, 51
    relentless practice of desired changes, 75–77, 131
    resources and personnel, 59–60, 111
    shared responsibility, 74, 82, 103, 130
    systems of meaning, 116–117
    undergraduate and graduate involvement, 68–69, 127
    web site, 4, 86
East St. Louis Community Action Network (ESLCAN), 68, 79

East St. Louis Community Development Block Grant Operations Corp., 68
East St. Louis Neighborhood College, 3–4, 67–68, 76, 110, 129
Ellig, Jerry, 82, 83, 84, 85, 86
Emergencies. *See* Federal Emergency Management Agency (FEMA)
Emerson Park Development Corporation, 61–62, 79
Emerson Park Neighborhood Revitalization Plan, 71
Employees. *See also* Resources and personnel
    career employees, 35, 96
    culture's role for, 6
    empowerment of, 28–29, 75
    sharing responsibility, 48–49, 65–66, 74–75, 130
    training. *See* Training of employees
    worldview of, 9
Empowerment, 28–29, 75
Energy, Department of, 39
Environment. *See also* Integration
    autonomy within. *See* Autonomy
    creative thinking about, 134–136
    external influences, 28–33
    as factor in cultural change, 92–96, 104
    as factor in cultural roots, 54–57
    fragmented culture and, 27
    importance of, 25–27, 124
    intertwined with leadership, 33–34, 124–125
    local and regional influences, 117
    manager's understanding of, 112–117
    political environment, importance of, 96, 102, 134–135
    public vs. private sector, 136–137
ESLARP. *See* East St. Louis Action Research Project
ESLCAN. *See* East St. Louis Community Action Network
Esseman, Dean, 82, 106
Essence of culture, 88–92, 104
Evaluations of changes, 129–130
    CD–CP, 91, 129
    ESLARP, 4, 76, 87, 129
Executive Office of the President, 36
External influences. *See also* Environment
    by default, 28–30
    by design, 30–31
    by transplant, 31–33

Federal Aviation Administration, 123
Federal Deposit Insurance Corporation (FDIC)
    autonomy of, 92–95, 104

Federal Deposit Insurance Corporation (FDIC) *continued*

changes to comply with consumer protection regulation, 30–31
commitment of, 49, 120
congressional influence injected in 1980s, 94–95
environment of, 92–95, 104, 136
field offices' differences, 117
Office of Consumer Affairs, 95
partners vs. competitors, 113–114
symbol and motivating belief of, 90
training of employees, 95
Federal Deposit Insurance Corporation Improvement Act (FDICIA), 94
Federal Emergency Management Agency (FEMA). *See also* Witt, James Lee
communication, 51, 57–58, 63–64, 77–78, 81, 82, 91, 131
cultural change of, 42, 80–82, 91
customer service approach, 72, 91, 129
customer survey by, 70
determining and articulating cultural change, 63–64
evaluations of changes, 129–130
existing culture, 50–52
external environment, efforts to manage, 72
information system, 69–70
institutionalizing change, 79–80
internal management of culture, 69–70
nature of task, 57–58
resources and personnel, 60–61
Senior Executive Service (SES) staff, 70
shared responsibility with employees, 75, 130
Federal Reserve Board (Fed)
autonomy of, 32, 34, 92–94, 104, 133
changes to comply with consumer protection regulation, 30–31
commitment to reasonableness, 93, 94, 118, 120, 121
information gathering to determine commitments, 118–120
resources available to, 45
responsiveness of, 40
sustaining culture, 133–134
Federal Reserve system. *See also* Federal Reserve Board (Fed)
customer of U.S. Mint, 115
partners vs. competitors, 114

Feldman, Martha, 39, 123, 138
FEMA. *See* Federal Emergency Management Agency
Fenno, Richard, 83, 108, 122
Fesler, James, 14
Fetterman, David, 122
Field research as method for studying existing culture, 47
Financial Institutions Recovery Reform and Enforcement Act (FIRREA), 94
Fiorina, Morris, 122
Floyd, Elson, 107
Formal accountability, 112–113
Fragmented culture and environments, 27
Framework for understanding organizational culture, 18–19, 42–87. *See also* Cultural roots
Frederickson, George, 123
Friel, Brian, 123

Gaebler, Ted, 14
General Accounting Office (GAO), 14, 60, 83, 84, 85, 112, 114
Glick, William, 38
Glidewell, John, 83
Goffee, Rob, 37, 38
Goldstein, Herman, 139
Gore, Al, 6, 13, 14, 123, 132
Government Performance and Results Act of 1993 (GRPA), 14, 123
Government reformers, 15, 34, 43
Grace, J. Peter, 36
Grace Commission. *See* President's Private Sector Survey on Cost Control
Greenspan, Alan, 94
"Groping along" type of management, 48
Gulick, Luther, 15, 36
Gusfield, Joseph, 40

Hargrove, Erwin, 83
Havrilesky, Thomas, 40
Heskett, James, 37, 38
Hill-Kennedy, Scott, 107
Hinchman, James F., 14
Hirsch, Paul M., 37
Hollings, Ernest, 58
Hoover, Herbert, 36
Housing and Community Development Act of 1992, 56
Housing and Urban Development, Department of (HUD), 56, 68, 76, 84
Huber, George, 38
Hummel, Ralph, 40

Ikenberry, Stanley O., 54
Industries' influence on culture, 31–33
Information gathering, 51–52, 117–120. *See also* "Soaking and poking" method of research
Ingersoll, Virginia, 29, 40
Ingram, Helen, 139, 140
Institutionalizing change, 78–80, 101–103
Integration
    of commitments to influence and shape culture, 43
    culture as integrating force, 18–22
    of tasks, resources, and environment, 43, 45–48, 53, 94, 125
Internal and external management of culture, 34, 48–49, 66–73. *See also* Resources and personnel

Japan vs. U.S. for competitive advantage, 18, 20
Jones, Gareth, 37, 38
Jorgenson, Danny, 122

Kaufman, Herbert, 25, 39, 96, 97, 106
Kennedy, Allen A., 13, 37, 38, 39
Kettl, Donald, 14, 38, 40, 122, 140
Khademian, Anne, 38, 39, 40, 83, 106, 107, 122, 123, 138
Knott, Jack, 13
Kotter, John, 37, 38
Kreps, David, 37, 38

Labor unions and universities, 102–103
Landis, James, 22, 23, 101–102
Laswell, Harold, 85
Leadership
    building capacity to change, 131–133
    challenging established authority relations, 130
    creative thinking about environment, 134–136
    encouraging participation, 126–128
    evaluating changes, 129–130
    importance of, 22–24, 124
    intertwined with environment, 33–34, 124–125
    limited influence of, 96
    listening and learning, 125–126
    providing resources, 128–129
    public managers' role, 9
    public vs. private sector, 137
    relentless practice of desired changes by, 49, 75–78, 131

    responsibility for culture, 33–34
    shared responsibility, 48–49, 65–66, 74–75, 130
    successful leadership styles for cultural change, 105, 109, 125–133
    sustaining culture, 133–134
Learning cultures, 21
Lessons learned, 124–136
Lipsky, Michael, 14, 139
"Listen and learn" as part of leadership style, 125–126
Local and regional influences, 117
Louw, Antoinette, 106
Luke, John, 85

MacDonald, Douglas, 82, 106
Malan, Mark, 106, 107
Management. *See* Leadership; Public managers and management
Map of program commitments and culture, 109, 121, 126
Marais, Etienne, 107
Marans, Steven, 74, 82, 83, 85, 86, 87, 106
Martin, Joanne, 36, 39, 40
Maslow, Abraham, 139
McGregor, Douglas, 139
Mental health partnership. *See* Child Development–Community Policing (CD–CP)
Merriam, Charles, 36
Metcaff, H., 139
Meyer, John W., 40
Miller, Gary, 13, 38, 139
Mineta, Norman, 58
Mint, U.S., 45, 115
Moe, Terry, 41, 85
Moore, Mark, 14, 41, 140
Moran, Mark, 122
Mosher, Frederick, 85
Mufamadi, Sydney, 98, 101

Nadler, G., 38
Nagler, Steven, 82, 106
National Academy of Public Administration (NAPA), 50, 83
National Aeronautics and Space Administration (NASA), 32–33, 45–46
National Partnership for Reinventing Government, 86
National Performance Review, 13, 123, 132
National Project to Reinvent Government (NPR), 6
Neighborhood College. *See* East St. Louis Neighborhood College

Neighborhood Technical Assistance Center
(NTAC), 68, 86
New Haven Department of Police Service,
52–53, 58–59. *See also* Child Development–Community Policing (CD–CP); Pastore, Nicholas
cultural change, 42, 91
determining and articulating cultural
change, 64–65
internal management of culture, 66–67
training of police officers, 128
web page of, 83
Nixon, Richard, 36
NPR (National Project to Reinvent Government), 6
NTAC. *See* Neighborhood Technical Assistance
Center

Office of Management and Budget, 112
Office of Personnel Management, 114
Office of the Comptroller of the Currency
(OCC), 114, 115
changes to comply with consumer pro-
tection regulation, 30–31
commitment of, 120
vague mandate of, 93
Office of University Partnerships, 84
Osborne, David, 14
Ott, J. Steven, 13, 36, 89, 106
Ouchi, William G., 13, 14, 37, 38

Participant observation, 108. *See also* "Soaking
and poking" method of research
Participation, leaders to encourage, 126–128
Partnerships, 91, 113, 121, 127. *See also* Child
Development–Community Policing
(CD–CP)
distinguishing competitors from partners, 113–114
Pastore, Nicholas. *See also* Child Development–Community Policing (CD–CP);
New Haven Department of Police Service
assessment of existing commitments,
52–53, 58
cultural change brought about by, 43,
80–82
determining and articulating cultural
change, 61, 64–65
environment of program, understanding of, 135–136
external environment, efforts to change,
73

institutionalizing change, 79
internal management of culture,
66–67
leadership style of, 125–133
"listen and learn" approach of, 126
participatory approach of, 127–128
relentless practice of changes, 78, 131
statements by, 83, 86, 87, 139
training of personnel by, 128
Peach, J. Dexter, 84
Perrow, Charles, 139
Persistence, 34–35
Personnel. *See* Resources and personnel
Peters, Thomas, 13, 37, 38
Police. *See* Child Development–Community
Policing (CD–CP); New Haven Department of Police Service; South African Police
Service (SAPS)
President's Committee on Administrative Management, 15, 36
President's Private Sector Survey on Cost Control (Grace Commission), 13, 36
Production of culture, 44–47
Professionals' influence on organizations' culture, 31–33
Progressive reformers, 6, 15
Public managers and management. *See also* spe-
cific government agencies
ability to bring about change, 96
adoption of business terminology by,
31
autonomy of. *See* Autonomy
commitments of, 16
compared to private sector, 136–137
culture in, 5–12, 44–47, 137–138
distinguishing between belief systems,
89
influencing and shaping culture by integrating commitments, 43
insights for, 33–35
leadership role of, 9, 33–34, 137–138
as participant observers, 108
persistence and follow-through, 34–35
policy analytic offices, 31
political environment, importance of,
96, 102, 134–135
responsibility for culture, 33–34
short-term nature of positions, effect of,
35

"Quality cultures." *See* Total Quality Management (TQM)

"Quantitative" organizations, 29
Questions unanswered, 136–137

Rabe, Barry, 14
Rainey, Hal, 38, 39
Randall, Richard, 82, 106
Rauch, Janine, 106
Reagan, Ronald, 36
Reardon, Kenneth. *See also* East St. Louis Action Research Project (ESLARP)
  cultural change brought about by, 2–3, 10, 42, 80–82
  determining and articulating change, 61, 62
  environment of program, understanding of, 135
  identifying why project was failing, 51, 56
  internal management of culture, 67–69
  "listen and learn" approach of, 125
  management style of, 11, 76, 125–133
  participatory approach of, 91, 127, 130
  relentless practice of changes, 75–77, 131
  resources and personnel provided by, 128–129
  sharing of responsibility fostered by, 74, 130
  university participation, attempts to change, 71, 121, 127, 130
  writings and statements by, 12, 82, 83, 84, 85, 87, 107, 122, 139
Reformers, 6, 28. *See also* Government reformers; Progressive reformers
Regional influences, 117
Reich, Robert, 41
Reinventing Government, 5
Relentless practice of desired changes, 49, 75–78, 131
Resources and personnel. *See also* Employees
  failure to promote project's success, 59–61
  importance of leadership to provide, 128–129
  integration with tasks and environment, 43, 45–48, 53, 125
  internal management of, 66–70
  manager's identification of, 111
Roberts, Alasdair, 83, 85, 86, 87
Robustness of culture, 20, 21
Romzek, Barbara, 40, 82, 140
Roots of culture. *See* Cultural roots

Rourke, Francis, 40
Russell, E., 36

SAPS. *See* South African Police Service
Schachter, Hindy Lauer, 123
Schaefer, Mark, 82, 106
Schein, Edgar, 13, 14, 18–20, 37, 38, 39, 88–90, 105, 139
Schneider, Anne, 140
Schneider, Sandra, 83
Scientific management, 6
Scott, Esther, 106
Scott, Richard, 37, 39, 40
Securities and Exchange Commission (SEC), 22–24, 101–102
Selznick, Philip, 13, 26, 36, 39
Senge, Peter, 38, 139
Shad, John, 23–24, 102
Shafritz, Jay, 36
Shared responsibility, 48–49, 65–66, 74–75, 76, 82, 130
Shaw, Mark, 106
Shields, Thomas, 87
Skeptics toward culture as management tool, 24–33, 124
Smircich, Linda, 37, 105
Smith, Damon Y., 86
Smith, Steven Rathgeb, 14, 139
"Soaking and poking" method of research, 47, 51, 108–109, 118, 126
Social Security Administration, 39, 83
South African Police Service (SAPS), 97–101, 104, 134
  background, 97–98
  cultural roots on which to build, 100–101, 104
  obstacles to cultural change, 98–100, 104
Spear, S., 139
State Department, 26–27
Stone, Deborah, 40
Stories told, 47. *See also* Artifacts in organizational culture
Strategies of managing for change, 47–49, 105
Strength of culture. *See* Robustness of culture
Structure as key to good government performance, 15
Symbols, 23, 28. *See also* Artifacts in organizational culture
  FDIC example, 90, 93
  identification of, 47
  integration role in environment, 27

SEC examples of symbolic behavior, 23–24
Systems of meaning, 28–30, 116–117

Tasks
    integration with resources and environment. *See* Integration
    manager's understanding of, 110–111
    nature of, 57–59
Taylor, Frederick, 6, 13
Terry, Larry, 41
Theory Z, 20
Total Quality Management (TQM), 5, 28
Townsend, Patrick, 139
Training of employees
    FDIC, 95
    FEMA, 129
    New Haven Department of Police Services, 128
Trice, Harrison, 38, 39, 41
Tshwete, Stephen Vukile, 97, 99–101, 104, 134

Unanswered questions, 136–137
Universities and labor unions, 102–103
University of Illinois, 1–5, 68. *See also* East St. Louis Action Research Project (ESLARP)
    Cooperative Extension Service, 114
Urban Extension and Minority Access Project (UEMAP)
    Note: In 1992, this project's name was changed to the East St. Louis Action Research Project (ESLARP) and all entries are indexed under that name.
Urban renewal program. *See* East St. Louis Action Research Project (ESLARP)
Urwick, L., 139
U.S. Mint, 45, 115

Values and beliefs in organizational culture, 18, 19
Vision, 21, 48

Warwick, Donald, 39, 41
Waterman, Robert, Jr., 13, 37, 38

Wearing, Melvin, 82, 106
Weber, Edward, 14
Weingast, Barry, 122
Wilkins, Alan, 13, 37
Wilson, James Q., 14, 39, 106
Wilson, Woodrow, 40
Winstanley/Industry Park Neighborhood Improvement Plan, 71, 79
Witt, James Lee. *See also* Federal Emergency Management Agency (FEMA)
    assessment of existing commitments, 50–52
    cultural change accomplished by, 42, 80–82
    determining and articulating change, 63–64
    environment of program, understanding of, 135
    external environment, efforts to manage, 72
    information gathering by, 51–52, 125–126
    institutionalizing change, 79–80
    internal management of culture, 69–70
    leadership of, 82, 109, 125–133
    participatory approach of, 127, 130
    relentless practice of changes, 77–78, 131
    shared responsibility with employees, 75, 130
    training of personnel, 129
    writings and statements by, 83, 85, 86, 87, 122, 138
Woolley, John, 40
Worth, Robert, 85

Yale University Child Studies Center, 52, 58. *See also* Child Development–Community Policing (CD–CP)
    cultural change, 42–43
Yoder, Eric, 122
Younge, Wyvetter, 1, 13, 51, 54, 57, 110